I Feel Love

Notes on Queer Joy

Edited by
Samantha Mann

Thank you for reading! xx

Esther Mollica

Published by

Read Furiously

Read Often. Read Well.

Published by Read Furiously. First Edition.

ISBN: 978-1-7371758-7-2

Essay Collection
LGBTQ+ Literature
Anthologies
Queer Identity

For more information on *I Feel Love: Notes on Queer Joy* or Read Furiously, please visit readfuriously.com. For inquiries, please contact samantha@readfuriously.com.

Read (v): The act of interpreting and understanding the written word.

Furiously (adv): To engage in an activity with passion and excitement.

Read Often. Read Well. Read Furiously!

"Anyway, whatever it is, don't be afraid
of its plenty. Joy is not made to be a crumb."

–Mary Oliver
"Don't Hesitate"

***

Names and identifying markers have been changed in all works

Table of Contents

Foreword

Samantha Mann

"Don't you think it's wild?" I asked my uncle over a glass of wine as we lounged around a firepit in my parents' backyard. It's December, but in Phoenix that means prime outdoor lounging weather. "Like, I am legally married, and I am literally holding my son who does not have an ounce of my DNA and nonetheless my name is emblazoned across his birth certificate along with Alissa's. I took 8 weeks of Paid Family Leave in the state of New York as maternity leave. Right, it's crazy?" My uncle had married his partner some 30 years after they started dating when California legalized civil unions around 2006.

"It's the way it's supposed to be," he said taking a gulp of wine and making a silly face to my smiling son. His casualness was grating.

Alissa and I married in 2016, one year and one month after the Supreme Court declared same-sex marriages legal as defined by federal law and declaring civil unions separate and unequal. The queer legal ease of my life has astounded me and often leaves me with a deep-rooted sense of survivor's guilt. When I came out it was to minimum fanfare in my family, everyone already knew and loved Alissa. My parents had already secretly whispered to themselves about the possibility of my sexual orientation for years. Sure, I had harbored personal shame and anxiety about being out, it's something that continues to tug to varying degrees even today, but the general smoothness of my queer experience is a marvel that I don't know how to reconcile with the history of violence and marginalization against the community.

During his twenties, my uncle starved himself, emotionally and physically. For a long time, examining his sexuality was too much for him to bear yet alone accept, so like many queer people his body took the brunt of his shame. Looking at pictures of him from that time, he is hollowed out, clearly starved. Starved of self-acceptance, confidence, and empty of thoughts about the possibility of a hopeful future. This was the early 90s, not some far-off time or place. Queer folks have spent centuries, eons, losing their family, friends, and lives due to their sexual and gender identities and here I am waltzing around with a federally legal marriage certificate and touting around my baby, creating branches on our family tree.

The ostentation of it all! A tree and branch that a mere 30 years prior might not have existed at all. I think a lot about missing family trees and branches. Picturing a forest full of stumps, all erased, invisible, and never allowed to begin to grow causes my stomach to drop, feeling sick.

I'm mad every time I learn something new about queer culture, how could I have not known about the Daughters of Bilitis? I quiz my wife when we watch

TV and shove tidbits of knowledge into her brain when I can, feeling like it's the least I can do to make sure we know who we came from and why we have the rights we have. It never feels like enough. I feel guilty having this life and not knowing how to honor the people who came before, the ones who fought, the ones who died, the ones who lived in social isolation to be with their lovers, the ones who lived and died closeted without experiencing life in the open as their truest self, and the millions who suffered silently. I haven't done anything to deserve the queer life I have.

I am shocked when I try to explain all of this angst to my uncle, who has lost too many friends due to AIDS and lives in a country where his relationship was not seen as legal until he was the ripe age of 50.

"It's just the way it's supposed to be, your life feeling easy is the whole point," he stated again ensuring me there is no expectations of me to be indebted, other than to live my life as I see fit.

The media representation of queer culture has come a long way, but joy is an area where more attention needs to be paid. Our depicted stories are often focused on trauma and hardship, but that is not the magic of queer people; most humans have stories of loss and longing. While media representation concentrates on queer stories surrounding this pain they do so at the expense of breezing past the magic. Because of historical social obstacles and our traumatic pasts, queer people are capable of experiencing and appreciating depths of joy unknown to most. We have an ability to uncover joy in surprising places. Queer people know joy can be fleeting and when we have it, we scoop it up with our bare hands, devouring it like a child placed in front of cake, swallowing it whole, not leaving a crumb behind, not a fork in sight.

Queer researcher and psychologist Dr. MacCrate stated, "I think queer people are good at responding to things flexibly and creatively. A lot of our lives are made up, in a way. There hasn't been such a laid-out path for us to follow, so when things get hairy and we don't see a way ahead it feels like, 'oh, okay, we've been here before.'"[1] This ability to create something from nothing and imagine opportunities never offered *is* the magic.

We are creators, even if only by existing as ourselves.

This collection was put together with love and joy and is sent out as an offering. We honor our past by celebrating and appreciating present moments of joy, whether it's all encompassing or merely a single ember burning in the dark. We will take it whenever we can and allow it to live inside us as often as possible. The collection is assembled as an attempt to make up for years of lost oral story-telling, both passed down in family generations and that missing from mainstream publications and outlets.

The realization that today family trees of variant types are blossoming at a higher rate than ever before is a salve.

This collection is a flowering branch for us all.

---

[1]Mann, Samantha. "The Lesbians are Alright," October 8, 2020, *BUST*, https://bust.com/living/197709-the-lesbians-are-alright-covid.html.

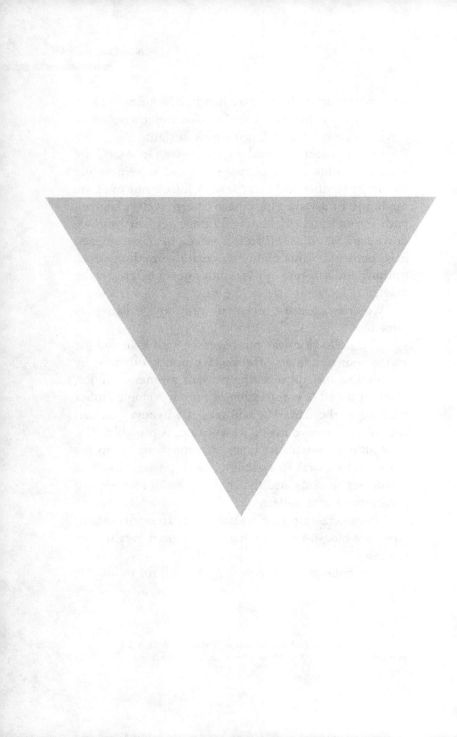

Something Happens in the Dark

John DeLamar

Something happens in the dark.

Something changes when the world transitions from garish fluorescence to silky darkness. For a moment you are held in the limbo of shuffling, shifting feet, the crackle of Ricola wrappers to nurse punctuating coughs, the low murmurs of whispered anticipation, and the nearly audible thump of a racing heart. For one moment you are held in the uncertain palm of the darkness, on the brink of magic.

. . .

As a child I was effeminate, with a little swish to my hips, a slight limp to my wrists, histrionic; I knew more about *Damn Yankees* than beer, babes, and baseball. I spent my childhood dodging the attention of my classmates, hoping to make it through a school day without a joke lobbed at my ponderous weight, my lisping, girly voice, the gentle way I ran the bases in kickball. Haranguing taunts of "run, titties!" and the not-so-hidden giggles from the sidelines shifted my labored gallop from a confidence building on base to an embarrassed amble, a stigmatizing out. I was the epitome of self-fulfilling prophecy. If there were a way to avoid human interaction, I found it, seized it, and broke free. I would lose the world around me as I wedged my nose in a book; I'd hide in my own shame at the back of the classroom; I'd return the small act of safe passage offered by teachers by clapping erasers. It was better to be alone – without a tribe – than to put myself in the path of confrontation.

When conflict was unavoidable and I was forced

face-to-face with the foes of my youth I saw the scene going down in a stylized ballet rumble, not with fists and blood. Instead of falling into the spaces between the metal bleachers with an absence of grace, I would turn with agile dexterity to stand tall against schoolyard thugs. Fantasies of theatrical strength ran deep under the tear-stained reality of narrowly avoiding an overabundance of fists and blood, laughing off the shoves on bleachers, or ignoring jeers that came when teachers' backs were turned. I counted the minutes to the final bell so I could get to the nights; so I could get to the dark.

The nights brought a surety, a sense of companionship, of belonging. Wrapped in the comfort of the night I would happily fall down the rabbit hole of Bette Davis's biting wit in *All About Eve*, howl at Lucille Ball's mad-cap attempts to get into show business, and whisper across the decades to her: "I understand." I would watch the Creature in James Whale's *Frankenstein*, see the pain in his misunderstood eyes, and wish there were a place where we could protect each other. Through classic films on VHS tapes borrowed from the local library – a deep sanctuary - to black and white sitcoms from a generation prior playing into the late hours of the night, I found a lifeline and a social genealogy of camp and metaphor. Long dead performers became my instructors, branches of a family tree I was constructing on my own.

Through these forays I found the glimmer and jazz of Busby Berkeley and the beauty of Fred Astaire and Ginger Rogers; wrapped in a pink blanket from my parents' linen closet, I would become Marilyn Monroe descending a staircase in *Gentlemen Prefer Blondes*. I was able to trace that legacy to Madonna, opening and building my cultural vocabulary. Liza Minnelli's Sally Bowles, with her fluid sexuality and her exaltation of love and life through strife, began to shape my worldview. In the erratic and captivating contortions of Bob Fosse and the dark subversions of Tim Curry I began to understand that those who live on the outside of the accepted have a people, a community, that lives in the shadows cast by stage lights; a world lit by magic.

In those dark nights I clung to magic's light.

. . .

Something happens in the dark.

Something breaks through when the velvet barrier of heavy drapery is pulled back, light floods the darkness, and the magic takes over. Then and now, now and then no longer matter; the glass and wood doors that hold back the real melt into the strange and exotic and, alarmingly, comfortable world unfolding on the boards. Fiction and reality blend and blur, one being replaced by the other until there is no way to determine which is truth. In the end, both maintain it.

. . .

I remember the first time I read *Angels in America*, and realized theatre was more than just simple artifice and glitter, it could be a testament to a people, a record of having been on this planet. Looking back at that young theatre student, scouring the department library for a play for a research paper, I can see the branches of my queer family tree bending to move my fingers to pick the beige spine tattooed with a single black "A" and a blue angel wing. All those difficult days and those nights of salvation had led me to this moment.

I was never one to read plays, believing their place was on the stage in full color, not in stark black on an off-white page. Plays and musicals were about people, real people, like me, not flat characters made of words. But, I read *Angels*, and I read it again, and I read it again. My copy now sits – battered and taped together – on my bookshelf, and every year I pick it up to remind myself of the importance of theatrical storytelling, of theatrical magic. The first time I read *Angels* was the first time I stopped watching worlds form and exist through performative theatrics, and became part of that world, really stepping into the time and place of the piece.

Angels in America changed the scope and purpose of my life.

I have made a point of seeing every production I can (professional and amateur), and the play continues to change my life. I have sat in the most uncomfortable of folding chairs to bear witness to the great work, scoured the internet to snag roughly edited snatches of college productions. It still brings unrelenting sadness and despair for a tribe of people who found me when I needed them, but also a thrilling joy that we have each other, that we have a shared culture of camp experience. It keeps the younger me close to my heart, it nurtures and protects him, and reminds him to look for magic.

During the most recent Broadway revival I was able to share the play with my husband and thousands of other gay men who flooded the plush seats of the Neil Simon Theatre. For one Saturday in 2019 I was able to take my husband's hand and walk into a sacred space with him, to have a communal moment with the tribe.

Magic met magic.

Sitting in that darkened theatre, with the lights playing across the stage, washing over the audience, my fingers twined between my husband's, that child who ran from the light got to smile, was allowed out to see a world that only existed in the realm of his imagination, that existed somewhere between the bugle beads, the jazz hands and face kicks; a world that was embedded in the glamour of pretend and the reality it sought to emulate and vanquish. That lisping, mincing, effete child of the black and white movie was allowed to hold the hand of a man he loved, get lost in the magic, and connect with his tribe.

. . .

Something happens in the dark.

Magic happens in the dark. The magic of watching a dream unfold before you; the magic of living a dream for others. The queer boy with the limp wrists, the swishing hips, the lispy voice puts his foot on the boards – he looks up to the boards – and the fear of the everyday, the tangles and foibles of being gay in a straight world, no longer exists. In the Neil Simon Theatre on that Saturday I found myself running from the dark to join the light. There was a unique gift of safety inside the darkness that only theatre could provide. I found myself running, not alone and not away, but partnered and toward something beautiful.

Permanent Record

Greg Mania

My relationship with my body is complicated, fluctuating between reluctant tolerance to welcoming demonic possession just to avoid dealing with it. This turbulent kinship operates in two capacities: on the surface and below. To which you might say, "Um, that is literally what having a body is." Yes, it is! AND IT'S A NIGHTMARE. What is a body if not a vessel for inconvenience and pain???? Truly, I can't think of a more severe punishment than being trapped in this ticking time bomb fashioned out of flesh, ready to ruin plans made well in advance with a migraine, or an IBS flare-up before boarding a flight. Other times, the flesh pouch in which I live ruins my day because the shirt I ordered did not fit like I thought it would, and every insecurity I've stuffed away like another pair of underwear into an already-full hamper comes flooding out. My body requires sex to be planned in advance; I need to prepare this rotting meat cage for another human to lick, suck, and/or fuck, and even then, when the moment comes, it might be off the table because of any number of reasons: from the physical (diarrhea) to the mental (catatonic depression), or both. There's no escape! If reincarnation is, indeed, real, I hope I come back as a gorgeous snake plant, because no matter what form I take, I will thrive in a low-lit, dry air-conditioned environment.

The first time I considered my body a threat, I was almost fourteen. When the other boys in my class were well on their way to developing deeper voices and facial hair, I was taking inventory of what I considered oddities compared to boys my age: my high-pitched voice, my lanky arms and legs, the vitiligo—which is a condition where skin loses its pigment cells, resulting in discolored patches—on my right arm. Every other boy in my class seemed to be light years ahead of me in the puberty Olympics, leaving me and my features considered feminine—which, back then, was a target on my back—behind. While I eventually, and finally, went through puberty myself (a week ago), my physical insecurities grew and changed with me. Even though I cultivated a style through an ostentatious wardrobe, I always felt unsatisfied once the clothes came off, the hair came undone, and everything else that became an extension of me was put away, ready to be used again the next day.

Most of my body dysmorphia—a common disorder in the queer community, especially among trans, genderqueer, non-binary, gender non-conforming, and other gender variant individuals—was a result of constantly comparing myself to other queer men, who were, more times than not, white, thin, and able-bodied. I was constantly barraged by—and ultimately rejected because of—messages like "no femmes," "masc only," and other similar dispatches on gay dating apps like Grindr, internalizing this disdain for the feminine from the very community I thought would embrace—and encourage!—it, enabling this nefarious display of toxic masculinity to disguise itself in the form of self-hatred. I spent most of my time trying to look like these boys, the ones that were always getting re-blogged on my crushes' Tumblrs, without realizing that I ultimately did not want to look like that at all, without knowing that there were other ways of being, looking, and existing.

A few years later I'd stop chasing these beauty standards, the ones that seemed to grant automatic access to the island of Mykonos, and I'd even embrace my femininity, tall hair, and gender-bending wardrobe. Despite this shift, I still nursed a low-grade insecurity when the artifice came off, when I was met with my naked body in the mirror. I never felt hot enough, thin enough, butt never tight enough, resulting in a message I transmitted back to myself over and over again: that I was never good enough.

. . .

I've wanted a tattoo ever since I laid eyes on Sporty Spice in 1998. I thought she looked so cool, brimming with confidence and secure in her sense of self. Her look, including her tattoos and nose ring, seemed like an extension of herself. I initially wanted a nose ring, too, but while that desire faded—I've opted to let dudes with nose rings ruin my life instead—my penchant for tattoos didn't.

I didn't seriously start thinking about what I wanted to ink in permanence on my body until I was nineteen or twenty. A lot of my friends at that age—especially my friends in New York City nightlife—were covered, which made me feel naked. I'm not saying I felt a pressure to conform—by the way, tattoos on the whole aren't, nor have they ever been, a trend???? People have been getting inked since, like, the wheel was invented, babe!—but it did reinforce my desire to use my body as a medium for expression. This may sound morose, but I like the idea of being buried with something of permanence that has brought me joy in life. I started thinking about what I wanted to get tattooed first. Shout-out to past Greg for not going through with ninety-nine percent of those ideas, because they were embarrassing! As in going into a tattoo shop on the Jersey boardwalk, closing my eyes, and pointing to the first one on the wall embarrassing. My best friend, Ky, has "Gimme" on the side of one palm and "Danger" on the side of the other, and the first tattoo I seriously considered getting was "Search and Destroy" in the same places, because we used to drive around Brooklyn in my Honda Civic, screaming to Iggy and the Stooges with no fewer than fourteen cigarettes dangling out of our mouths.

But my first tattoo, a few years later, in 2018, erred more towards the sentimental.

. . .

Daffodils were my favorite flowers growing up. We had multiple gardens of them in our yard. My dad and I used to walk through the woods surrounding our house with shovels and plastic bags in hand, digging up wild daffodils to bring back to plant in one of our gardens. They come in a variety of colors, but my favorite was always yellow (my favorite color, which, at that age, was my obsession: I wanted a yellow Volkswagen Beetle, my room and toys were all yellow, I only drew on the sidewalk in yellow chalk, everything yellow, yellow, yellow, and...not much has changed actually. Have you seen the cover of my first book?) and I'd always liked how goofy they looked to me, like giant trumpets. I loved how animated they were. They had a big personality; they instilled a sense of wonder in seven-year-old me by standing out in the garden, exuding pure, unfettered joy.

As an adult, I wanted to find that joy again, so at twenty-eight I started gardening—an actual hobby, which, in any other case, would make me break out in hives because my hobbies are strongly limited to re-runs of *Top Chef* and Advil PM. But I found respite in visiting my parents' house, only an hour and a half away from my apartment in Brooklyn, and claiming my own spot in the yard that I had once learned how to ride a bike in. I selected an area that received the right amount of light, prepared it with the right soil and appropriate fertilizer, and watched the bulbs I ordered bloom. There are literally a million different types of daffodils—each belonging to the genus *narcissus*—and they can be white, pink, red, green, orange, tall, small, trumpet, ruffled trumpet, no trumpet, but I went for the classic. My daffodils—ordered directly from Holland because I COMMIT (to being extra)—are called "Dutch Masters," tall and strong, with muted-yellow petals and a trumpet a few shades darker, yielding a striking contrast as the sun goes down.

It was one particular night in 2018, when I was sitting out back in the yard, during a spring weekend I was visiting my parents and jolly blooms, that I made the decision to finally get my first tattoo. So I sat on a patio chair, bullshitting on my phone, deciding which tattoo I wanted to get. I was leaning towards "Search and Destroy" until I looked up and saw my first tattoo staring right at me. Like, hello, duh, of course. I didn't even hesitate. I emailed my friend's tattoo artist and booked an appointment.

A few weeks later, I went to a studio in Williamsburg to get my daffodil tattooed. I went alone after work one day and waited in the lobby after filling out some consent forms. I wasn't nervous about getting the actual tattoo, needles don't bother me; I was more anxious about my body pulling one of its notorious stunts, like OF COURSE my body would reject the ink and I would break out in hives, or it wouldn't even be tattoo-related, my appendix would just spontaneously burst then and there, right in front of these Ultra-Cool Tattooed People. Embarrassment hides behind every corner!

Surprisingly, for me, it couldn't have been smoother. I bonded with my tattoo artist, Virginia, over our mutual friends and books. She was patient and kind, explaining every step of the process, and when the time came to put needle to skin, it was tolerable, not much more than a mild discomfort. Of course, I was getting tattooed on my arm, a relatively low-pain area. If I was getting tattooed on my ribs, well, RIP.

I left an hour later with a daffodil—in black ink only, a motif I've continued to employ with my tattoos going forward—above my left elbow. I couldn't stop looking at it, smiling every time I caught it in the mirror, this little spot on my body becoming my new favorite body part.

I finally liked what I saw.

The mirror became less a source of dread and more a celebration of this little plot of joy on my body, a reminder that one day that plot, like my garden, can grow and, ultimately, flourish.

. . .

LOL. THAT'S A NICE SENTIMENT, ISN'T IT? And I believed it for a few weeks until my body decided to kick it into high gear with yet another betrayal. This fucking anatomical Judas is just a conveyor belt, churning out one malady after another. In 2018, the same year I started getting tattooed, I was playing Whac-a-Mole with a diagnosis for a nebulous bowel syndrome.

I've always had a chronically weak GI tract but in the past few years it had gotten even worse, eventually reaching a fever pitch in 2018. It'd always been easier to dismiss it as a "weak stomach" or "nerves," which, yes, duh, everything gives me anxiety, and my stomach and bowels react accordingly (abdominal pain and diarrhea, respectively). But, after way too many close calls just sitting there, minding my own business, like on the fucking G train and then having to run upstairs at the next stop and dash into the bathroom at a Korean BBQ place like an Olympic sprinter, I decided to finally see a gastroenterologist.

And so I embarked on a long road of tests, tests, and more tests, each trying to determine what it isn't. I tested negative for colon cancer, Crohn's, and ulcerative colitis; I shit in fucking boxes and dropped them off in labs; I took hours-long breath tests to identify any possible lactose, sorbitol, or fructose malabsorption. I became extremely depressed from how lonely and isolating the whole experience was. I stopped attending any social gatherings, leaving the house only to go to my part-time job in downtown Brooklyn. I stopped having sex with my partner for fear of a bodily emergency, the shame and anxiety of not knowing what's wrong with me rendering me a shell of a person. After growing up navigating one affliction after another—being hooked up to a nebulizer all night because of severe asthma as a child, lying in MRI machines in seventh grade to figure out the source of daily headaches—this one was the one that broke me.

What used to be a GI condition that I could alleviate by either staying home and letting the storm pass or by popping an anti-diarrheal had evolved into tip-toeing around a mine field. I never knew when my body would rebel against me, what occasions and moments it would ruin. By beating it to the punch and eradicating any activities that required me leaving the presence of a toilet, my depression worsened from the self-imposed isolation. The beach? No, thank you! A hike? LOL AT THINKING I WOULD EXPOSE MYSELF TO THE SCAM THAT IS THE "GREAT" OUTDOORS BY CHOICE EVEN IF MY BOWELS WEREN'T TRASH! (I'm sorry, but you ever been in the woods? It's a booby trap disguised as a place to "clear your head." By clear your head, do you mean GET LYME? Can't we just look but not touch?) Even taking a train ride gave me anxiety. Having people over? My roommate would be like, "Let's have a house party!" First of all, why would you want anyone in your home ever???? And more than two people and one toilet? I think not!

Eventually, my GI doctor diagnosed me with a small

intestinal bacterial overgrowth, SIBO for short, which is an abnormal increase in the bacteria population of the small intestine. This overpopulation is exasperated by certain foods and liquids, and the road to remission is a long one: First, I was prescribed antibiotics the size of a pet's tombstone that I had to take three times a day for two weeks. Then, I had to go on an elimination diet, a months-long process which, in the end, proved futile. For the most part. My triggers are always changing, and my IBS just seems to flare-up whenever it feels like it. There's also the risk of more bacterial overgrowth, so it makes differentiating between IBS and another bacterial overgrowth difficult, because guess what? I STILL GET DIARRHEA ALL THE TIME.

. . .

If my body was going to rebel against me, I was going to rebel against it. I decided to take back control by getting more tattoos up in this bitch.

My next two were a (small) pair: an inverted triangle on my left index finger, and a small thunderbolt on my right. I got these two a few months after I got my first tattoo. It just seemed like a given: a symbol for queerness and an ode to David Bowie. LOW HANGING FRUIT, I KNOW. But more than that, it was a visceral reaction to my unruly body; it was a way for me to exercise choice, to have agency over myself again. It was a way to find pleasure from my body, to stop thinking of it as an enemy and instead as a canvas for possibility.

A few months later, towards the end of 2019, I landed the opportunity to fly out to Los Angeles to pitch a pilot that I wrote and meet with a handful of managers and agents for possible representation. As Miley sings in "Party in the U.S.A.", I hopped off the plane at LAX with my dream and Imodium. I got in my rental car and drove from meeting to meeting, pitching my pilot filled with stupid jokes to development executives and producers, all while praying to all that is holy that I don't shit my pants in LA traffic, or worse, right in the room while I try to get the development executive behind *This Is Us* to care about a comedy based on my sad, gay life.

It was the sweatiest, nerve-wracking week I've ever had, and eventually, in 2020, I signed with two managers with whom I met and clicked with in October. But, while I was in LA, I wanted to remember the experience, because even if this pilot never gets made, it brought me from my Lexapro Lodge in Brooklyn to a reasonably priced Airbnb in Hollywood, and into meetings with people responsible for some of today's biggest shows on TV. And if my stupid jokes aren't immortalized on the big screen, one of them would be immortalized on my forearm.

In a scene in the pilot, the eponymous protagonist, Greg, and his best friend, Toni, are at Party City, bartering for a fog machine. Toni, a tattoo artist, eventually convinces the cashier to give them the fog machine in exchange for free ink up to the amount the fog machine is priced at. He agrees, and the tattoo he wants is a seahorse, which is what I got done the day before I flew back to New York.

While the seahorse (which also happens to be another childhood obsession of mine that comes in yellow) signifies a turning point in my life and career, it is also a reminder that I am more than my physical limitations and insecurities, that my body, TRY AS IT MIGHT, sabotage any physical or mental equilibrium I attempt to achieve, I still—despite and in spite of it—chose possibility over quiescence. As much as I dragged my feet, held on to any object I could get a firm grasp of in an effort to delay doing literally anything that isn't rotting on my couch watching *Charmed*, I went and did it anyway.

. . .

I just got an old-school Volkswagen key tattooed on my forearm, near the seahorse. My dad had, like, eight Beetles when he was younger, and I always wanted a—you guessed it—yellow one. My next appointment is already scheduled. I'm getting my literary tattoo: Ramona THE Pest, my tantrum queen, from the beloved and iconic *Ramona* children's book series by Beverly Cleary. I can't think of a better fit for me. I want to get Storm from the X-Men with her eighties-era mohawk, smoking a cigarette on my outer thigh. There will probably be more, and although I'm not sure what or where they'll be, I'm excited to find out.

My ideas for tattoos shift and change, but their purpose remains the same.

They are symbols of joy—of past, present, and future—and also rebellion. They are a symbol of the choice to carve a space for myself, even within my physical confines. Also, which of these tattoos am I ever going to regret? Do you really think that one day I'm going to slam down my cup of Metamucil and be like, FUCK DAFFODILS, HO. I'm not going to wake up one day and not be queer anymore. Why would I develop a sudden disdain for seahorses? I know that's rich coming from me—someone who can find a disdain for anything!—but a seahorse tattoo is highly unlikely to stir regret in me, especially given the meaning ascribed to it.

My tattoos are a record of my past and a host for my future joy in which, no matter what fucked-up shit I go through, offers, at the very least, the comfort of a pleasant memory. They are access points to the rediscovery of my body, little permissions to look in the mirror and come to appreciate the totality I was born with. Tattoos have helped me to reclaim myself, my selfhood. And with that comes finding joy in a place where none used to be. My body, with all its (mal) functions, started to feel like less of a discrepancy in personhood, and more like a plant that needs nurturing and care. Like the perennial I have above my elbow, I hope I always come back—to myself.

On Being Same-Sex Attracted

Danny Roy

Within my first year of puberty, it started to become increasingly difficult to write a single honest journal entry. Virtually every time I'd pick up my pencil, I'd dwell on secret thoughts I wanted to scribble down, then feel this nagging fear I'd die tomorrow and all of my secrets would be carried across the wind like the seeds of a tumbled dandelion stem. Today I am the steward of a large storage Tupperware of journal notebooks that document many less then enthralling accounts of "today was just okay."

Like many queer folks, I was developing in a closet and practiced the art of pretend daily. This habit penetrated every aspect of my existence. My tendency for half-truth telling enabled the belief that I actually had the power to control what others think of me. There was no appreciation for the counterbalance of doubt, so I subscribed to whatever my authorities told me with complete allegiance. If I couldn't get others to see me as straight, I'd get someone else to tell me how to be straight. I might have carried on pretending forever—but by the age of 23, I was beginning to feel extreme pressures from church leaders to marry, and this was one feat (despite many attempts) I couldn't seem to falsify my way through. So one evening, I courageously admitted to myself that I was probably homosexual *enough* to voluntarily enter Mormon reparative therapy.

Mormons could not have designed a better dating service for gay men than their take on reparative therapy in the early aughts. "Evergreen" was the name of this particular iteration of therapy, and it consisted of roughly a ten-member batch of traumatized men exiled to a secret corner of a building, in a low-lit room, hatched between the hours of 6-8pm on Wednesday evenings.

If I had enrolled 15 years earlier, chances are much higher I would have endured electroshock therapy at BYU. In that way, it feels a bit like I won the strangest of jackpots. My Mormon therapist had informed me prior to joining the group that the therapy functioned in a sort of accountability fashion, members came together to discuss their sexuality "temptations" through the filter of principles we would acquire through lessons. I was also discouraged from using identity terms like "gay" and "homosexual" and told to practice using "same-sex attraction" or "same-gender attracted" in their stead. *Ahhh,* I thought to myself immediately, *I'm not actually "gay," I'm same-sex attracted!*

These meetings were led by two straight church leaders, though at the true helm of our group is the handsomest of kings, kwains and captains: The Lord and Savior Jesus Christ, whose whiteness and glory defied all obstacles. Mormons have a relentlessly benevolent take on this man, who is considered a separate being from God the Father. To this day I'm unable to write about "Him" without the nuanced worship of a capital H for His every pronoun—as I had always been taught. He is by all accounts the perfect Son, unending in his forgiveness, sacrifice and patience. But even more importantly, He is considered the ultimate example of what every saint should aspire to become.

. . .

"Is anyone sitting here?" I asked a timid 20-something with red hair and acne.

I couldn't bear to make eye contact with him, but he grabbed the sides of his metal chair and moved a single millimeter, out of polite nervousness.

"uh..no go ahead."

Do I think he's cute? Occurred to me as I took my seat and looked around the room in slow, small sips. *Oh Heavenly Father, please don't let anyone I know in real life be here.* This is the more terrifying of the 2 thoughts.

Two seemingly straight men enclose the front of the circle. The grandfatherlier of the leaders is the last to sit and looks around the circle with a warmth that felt a tinge pitying.

"Brethren, we are so glad you are here" he starts, "Each of you has been blessed, with one of the greatest struggles known to man, and we support you in your righteous desire to stay close to the Lord, and diminish your same-sex attractions. Let's go around the circle and check in. We do have some new members, so if each of you can introduce yourself, or share something about your struggles since we last met. A reminder that everything shared in this group is confidential and that we value speaking as righteous priesthood holders under the Lord."

From there the confessions began to flow in counterclockwise fashion. I was initially shocked to hear the other men speak so explicitly about aspects of their sexuality with Jesus's countenance adorning at least 3 of the 4 beige walls of that meeting room. These men would talk about things I'd thought of as taboo, such as pornography, or the number of times you masturbated that week (or didn't-yay!), one man with 6 children discussed the pains of an ongoing illicit affair. As tears fill his eyes, the neighbor seated next to him would reach over and pat him on the back. *We can touch each other here?!* I screamed silently to myself. It was a cacophony of tensions and within 45 minutes or so, I was fully enraptured in the seismic dramas of the group.

When it was finally my turn to speak, I was surprised by how ready I felt to join the fray. As I said my name, I leaned first backwards, then forwards in a compulsory move to get a degree of shame I felt to slither from my back.

"My name is Danny, and I'm struggling with same-sex attraction. I uhhh... I only recently tried masturbation for the first time in my life, which concerns me." I pause again. A clock somewhere in the room ticked, *and did one of the Jesuses just blink its eyes?* I gathered myself and began again. This time, the performer in me has returned and a false sense of confidence has filled me with story:

"I am full of sinful desires, and I can't seem to resist Satan's temptations, so I messed up recently. I uh. I masturbated. I completed the act quickly and it was awful, it didn't even feel good, because I knew I had displeased the Lord. I sing church hymns, now when I have those thoughts. And I'm here, so I guess that's good."

After sharing this, I allowed myself some relief, not a soul seemed surprised or disgusted by my struggle, which was nearly impossible for me to believe. *So, it's just someone else's turn now?* Someone else in the room began to speak, and my mind wandered deeper.

My not masturbating until the age of 23 *was* an incredible display of faithfulness, though I'd had a lot of help from our family pediatrician who asked me at the age of 11:

"Derek, do you know what masturbation is?"

I didn't, but I nodded, because he was pointing at my dick.

"And do you practice masturbation Derek?"

I shook my head shyly, but firmly "No."

Um Okay, what exactly was Mayor Nation? —I wondered, mishearing the word.

"Good" he uttered authoritatively, "because if you play with 'it,' 'it' will break."

I imagined my penis snapping in two, and the thought of touching myself much at all was put away for the next decade. A shocking amount of nocturnal emissions ensued my teenage years.

Upon my returning home from my mission that I had begun a secret R rated movie ritual, and I suspect a daring rental of *Y Tu Mamá También* played a crucial role in the proverbial straw that broke the camel's back. Several nights post-viewing, I made up a homework excuse in order to bail on my friends and go back to my dorm to close the blinds and contemplate sinful acts.

My peachy bare ass pressed against the cold stony desk chair, as I sat studiously gazing upon my crotch in the florescent light. This was me considering the possibility of deliberately pleasuring my very own body for the first time.

I began, unsure if I was doing it right, and after a longish 5 minutes ensued my body startled me with a sudden shudder and arc. Somehow there was a horrible millisecond to imagine myself at the top of the plunge being trapped in that initial force of pleasure, a scratched record skipping in place. And then suddenly, utter collapse into relief and astonishment; instantaneously I was spent and sold.

My sin was in the first degree for certain—willful, premeditated, just BAD and to further worsen this breech, a sudden moment of honesty shattered my consciousness. My brain, my stupid toaster brain had apparently buried an image of Dean Cain's spandexed Superman ass somewhere deep in its recesses and shot the fantasy to the tip top of my conscious, setting my orgasm into motion. *Ugh, those thoughts again. I'm disgusting.* In my post-coital state, I looked at the clock, 6pm. My friends would have been heading to dinner by then. Better to skip it. Toasted, gay smut thoughts for dinner that night; and dang it, I am what I eat.

A shadowy figure began to come expressly into view, and I was in the room again. The exactness of this shape was slowed only by my insistence to perceive him surreptitiously through the periphery of my left eye. He was a slender creature, in horn rimmed glasses and a baseball cap, bright cotton orange jacket— intended for hunting, and a tight pair of jeans with patches on both kneecaps and bright red tennis shoes. The memory of this moment is often accompanied by association of the smell coils make on a space heater at their hottest, I may have been sitting next to one that evening in group, or was it related to that orange hunting jacket? My chest lurched forward to drink him in more from an angle. *Was he there all along?*

He looked like a "Desmond" or "Ambrose" to me, but I was ultimately surprised to learn he had more the kind of name that ranks within the top 100 of "most popular boys names" of the time, so he was a "Jared" after all. He was predictably an artist, and I mused a very talented one based on how he was dressed. His voice was masculine, but slightly higher pitched, musical even. It was in that moment I realized his speaking had returned my attention. He had selected one of the darker corners of the room slouched back on the couch in the circle to inhabit. There was no eye contact between us, and though we sat several seats apart, I imagined our knees coincidentally bumping as he raised his hand slowly to introduce himself. *You are my new favorite part of the group,* I treacherously thought to myself.

Many clinical interventions of Evergreen were informed by the thesis that same-sex attracted men never learned how to relate to men - especially their father - in healthy ways. This made complete sense to me at the time and provided a real concrete path forward to my treatment. Not to mention it was wonderful news to be told that I needed to have MORE time with men, not less.

After meetings, I started walking more slowly back to my car, hoping for an opportunity to strike up conversations with other men…or encounter Jared by happenstance. I was feeling passively bold. I'd tie my shoes, or feign I forgot my jacket in the meeting room, only to then pretend to realize it was tied around my waist. My most effective strategy, was when I finally walked up to Jared and blurted out:

"Did you know it's my Birthday next week?" in hopes he'd feel obligated to celebrate.

It was amateur hour, but he graciously got excited.

"That's great, we should go out to dinner and celebrate!"

Imaginary vapors from the pink glow steamed off my chest and back, and I coughed out a halted "YEAH! Dinner YOU and ME!"

Then suddenly, a pang of anxiety informing me I was dangerously close to breaking the rules of maintaining appropriate relationships outside of the group. I accepted that this was only going to work out if we angled this towards a more AA-sponsorship sort of dynamic. So, I called over another group member named Ryan and invited him to join us. Ryan seemed to consider the request for several moments, then responded with an unenthusiastic "sure."

Several days later we came together at my dorm room before heading to the restaurant for my birthday dinner. I asked my roommate to take a photo, commemorating what I now consider to be my first gay threesome. There was a discernible rush in draping my arm stealthily around Jared, engaging our first physical contact beyond a handshake. Ryan stood awkwardly to the left of me and beamed a toothy smile. The photo is one of my last non-digital takes, so it renders an asymmetrical awkwardness I wouldn't discover until a year later in a box of undeveloped film.

Waiting for group each week started to become a torture unto itself. All other matters began to fade into the background, including any desire to force myself on dates with women. It was like finally being able to drop the rope on both sides of a lifelong tug of war and fall fully forward on both sides and embrace my "same-sex attractedness." I started showing up to group more stylishly: American Eagle everything, with a couple slightly more expensive Hollister items. I fancied myself a budget Abercrombie and Fitch model and bought a hair gel that naturally bleached blond streaks into your hair over time. I painted my arms unnecessarily heavily in sunblock. This was my more masculine reimagining of the Victoria secret pear lotion. I'll also admit that I wanted the other men to imagine I tasted like a coconut. I started praying less and renting my secret R rated movies more. Learning that other guys were constantly struggling with jacking off, freed me to just start giving in to my urges, though I rarely confessed this to the group.

A fellow member of the group worked for a senior center, and I had heard they needed volunteers for meals-on-wheels routes. This was exactly the kind of appropriate structure I needed to develop a healthy relationship with men. So, Jared and I took one on together. Our route expanded across a sizeable portion of the valley, and so every Friday afternoon we collected the meals in an oversized insulated bag, and drove across copper colored wheat fields to various farmhouses. We would devise inside jokes and imagine the lives of our elderly friends on long leisurely drives.

During one drop off, a particularly ancient man asked us to follow him into his basement. Unwaveringly we descended, as the old man, waved a shaking hand at the light switch to illuminate an unfinished concrete catacomb teeming in piles and piles of deer antlers and animal trophies. I turned to Jared in amazement, and we stole a secret smile of incredulity as the man sauntered forward to shuffle some of the bones in a rattle-y show and tell. I asked supportive questions of the man's interest in hunting, betraying my fright. Jared seemed fine until we left the house 30 minutes later laughing in huge hoots in the car as we drove away

"WHAT WAS THAT? DUDE WHAT WAS THAT?"

"I DON'T KNOW, WHAT THE HECK"

"WE'RE LUCKY WE DIDN'T GET MURDERED, WHAT IF THOSE WERE HUMANS?"

"THEY WERE ANTLERS DANNY, I'M SURE THERE WEREN'T ANY HUMANS."

"I knowwwwww BUT STILL!!!"

We laughed until we cried, and then I thought of Jared old and gray. He'd probably have 6 kids by then, but we'd live next door to each other and maybe we'd be hunting buddies once the therapy started working more and we both developed a love for guns.

One night after having a "slip" with Internet pornography I dramatically drove my coaxial cable to Jared's house in the pouring rain and asked him to take it from me, along with a simple silver promise ring I purchased in Mexico during a high school band trip years before. It was the most sentimental thing I owned at the time and I wrote a letter accompanying the ring, promising him, myself and God that I would never, ever put our friendship at risk like that again.

"I know our friendship is compatible only to the degree that we stay righteous and move toward holy marriage between a man and wife."

He hugged me, we cried, we prayed, we recommitted ourselves to God and yes—it was way hotter than anything I had probably viewed with that fucking coaxial cable. Jared later wrote a song about the ring I gave him, which is part of his story to tell.

In the final days of October, we decided to dress as "each other" for Halloween. Jared bleached his hair to match my dirty blond locks and borrowed one of my favorite American Eagle shirts. I wore his orange hunting jacket and glasses. My 32-inch waist squeezed most erotically into the tightness of his size 30-inch pants with the patches—and I draped myself in the smell of his orange hunting jacket. We attended a party that night where I would meet all of his closest friends. I felt adult in ways only an adolescent can. It had something to do with being invited to parties in houses with real art hung on the wall—which you couldn't yet afford to buy for yourself.

Jared, an art student, was preparing a finals project, and asked me to pose for a painting. I came to his studio and sat with my shirt off, hands squeezing my stomach and hunched over in the strangest way. This was by his direction, and so I pressed and sucked my gut firmly in as he photographed my shape. The studio was too cold to be shirtless, and it felt taboo to remove my holy garments for such a matter as this, but of course, I was eager to be seen.

I would later come to visit him developing the painting several times over its progression. Once I snuck in the studio to surprise him and caught him painting my hand to Radiohead's "Hail to the Thief" album. I would later buy this album, because I imagined it held all the secrets to how he felt about me—only to discover it was maddeningly poetic and sophisticated for such a concrete mind like mine—was it good to be a "Wolf at the Door" to someone? "Sail to the Moon" seemed encouraging and decided that was probably the song that reminded him most of me.

The painting is long gone, but I will never forget the first time I saw it. My twisted body on 5-foot canvas, mostly faceless except a jowl and lower lip. This in my mind was Jared's way of telling the world our secret without yet betraying either of us. We were the only two people who knew the identity of this individual grabbing his gut in anguish. I was painted next to a curvy woman with red curly hair, that I recognized as one of his neighbors in the art studio. I didn't know the word "muse" at the time, but I felt the concept deeply in my body, whether or not that was his truth. I wholeheartedly believed that we could truly inspire the best of each other. We would protect each other in this silent acknowledgement—because there was no other safe way for two men falling in love in a small Mormon college town to have this any other way. For this singular experience in my life, he will always be my favorite artist.

Not too long after the finals show, Jared conceded that he liked me beyond friend feelings--and that our relationship was getting too close for our righteousness goals. He worried we would accidentally become physical. He sent me a difficult email ending our contact, and for two weeks we went cold turkey from seeing each other until opportunity knocked.

A couple of girlfriends offered a mutual invitation to join them for a sleepover at a family's timeshare and it was just too tempting for either of us to pass up. Despite a mountain of pillows, we had established between us heading into bed that night, our celibacy failed. I lay tensely on my side, knowing we were both awake and roiling like snakes beneath the blanket. The warmth of Jared's curious right hand glided across the top of my arm and slowly began to penetrate the tautness of my waistband; I grabbed my mouth for fear of expression, as I forcefully shot waves of premature orgasm into my garments and then halted in a muted tremble. I waited a moment, then turned to him and offered reverently "Do you want me to do it back to you?" and he nodded vigorously.

One of the more stunning surprises after this deflowering was that songs I had sung since childhood began to bloom and weave new understandings of exactly what the cost of love is for a person who really means it. It's not that I attribute all of what I was experiencing to a single orgasm, but more so to the perceptible defeat of a lifelong subsystem that had been holding everything in check. Jared's family was much more involved in his attempts to change his sexuality, and for a time, so was he quite fervently— though obviously conflicted. To my understanding, the news of our tryst upset his family and subsequently they became more actively involved in his abstinence, including monitoring his contact with me. For the remainder of the school year, we tried many more abstinence stretches, usually at about two to three week excruciating intervals, always to return to each other's arms desperate to experience intimate embrace again. Heartbreak was becoming an ongoing actuality for me, and I apparently wanted to meet the moment shirt off-pants down, naked.

I left reparative therapy behind after our very first sexual encounter without much guilt or regret for quitting. I admitted to myself that I liked having screwed up, and I was ready to screw up more. I started to let myself fantasize about marrying Jared, and naming all of our 6 children JaDan Jr. (a most excellent merger of our names), and then fall into deep sobs for hours at our ill-fated love as though I was actually dying. In one particularly difficult separation stretch from Jared I came out to my parents, because I couldn't do it alone anymore. They weren't fully ready for it, but it was as good a day as any and we started what would continue to be a long walk together. Ultimately, this would not be my last love, I was young, and would most definitely fuck again, perhaps even start writing in my journal again.

That first physical encounter at the time share was lipless—no kissing and before we cut ourselves off from each other for good, we agreed that making out seemed like something we should both experience at least once. We drove up into the mountains one winter night in my '94 Mazda Protegé and parked at the corner of a freshly snow plowed parking lot, near a popular trail I walked in the summertime. There were limited heating features in my car, so we rushed to the back, and pounced on each other, fogging up the windows, stripping our clothes and allowing our greedy hands to guide us. We were ferocious, until an abrupt row of headlights careened into the parking lot and stopped several spots away.

A door opened, and footsteps moved toward us. We heard a group of people just outside the car— their tone of voice implying they needed some sort of attention. We sat still for one moment "hey is there anyone in there?" hand printed streaks on both sides of the back windows said yes, but we sat completely still. Jared and I looked at each other for a moment, and then I suddenly moved a "shhh" finger to my lips and slowly climbed naked over the console into the front seat and started the car. I turned on the ignition, and then slowly reversed; I couldn't make much of their images through the steamed windows, I didn't care to. As we drove away, I heard a man yell "Hey wait a minute!"

I drove for 15 minutes with only a sweater pulled over my naked body, until I found another spot lower in the valley farmland, not far from the antler basement house. I pulled the parking brake, and climbed back over the console to Jared, our mouths locking together again with renewed passion. Hours later, with our lips fatigued and chapped, I pulled out the gallon of water I'd saved under the driver's seat for emergencies and took a swig before handing it to Jared. I reached across the console a third time and turned on the radio. When I conjure the memory, I always pretend "Sail to the Moon" was playing.

That evening, we pushed away the entire outside world, and I reaped the rewards of our reparative therapy. My feet had touched a path I could walk with long lasting faithfulness towards change. I had healed myself in the carnal pleasures of my first deep romantic kiss. I was converted to truth and the sensation of my cold back against the window, as my chest pressed against a warm, new Him.

Cause You Gotta Have Faith

Esther Mollica

"This one goes up your pussy, and this one goes up your ass!"

I stood there, mouth agape as Jodi, a ginger-headed butch in a leather jacket weighed two alien probes in each hand like the scales of justice, a cinnamon bush of armpit hair escaping from the edge of her sleeve.

This was my first date with a woman.

I was 18 and living in San Francisco. It was the year 2000, and I'd somehow survived Y2K (along with a family on the news that hoarded an entire lifetime supply of banana pudding in their basement.) Finally, after six months of going to Club Faith alone, somebody asked me out. I'd gone to Faith, an 18+ gay bar, every single Thursday by myself, hoping a woman would talk to me.

When I was a sophomore in high school, I knew by the fluttery feeling in my chest whenever I watched *Xena: Warrior Princess* on TV that there was probably something more than a platonic appreciation of her ability to wield a chakram or administer some form of Greek acupuncture to extract information from her enemies. I didn't know what else to do but explore these feelings and become a flaneur at Club Faith, the only bar I could get into. In an era, pre-online dating and post-AOL, it wasn't possible to go onto a dating site and meet a girl, swipe left or right on an app. At the time, people thought the idea of meeting a stranger online was creepy. Still, there was PlanetOut, a short-lived LGBT dating site that only had 3 lesbians in the tri-state area. I'd message one and the chat box would flicker: "A/S/L?"

As soon I typed, "18" I'd get, "Sorry, I'm 47," or

the chat would abruptly end, ejecting me into silence.

I went to Faith religiously each week, for nearly half of a year. The girls would give me sly stares and winks, but no one would approach. I'd made friends with a drag queen named HollyGram and a flamboyant twink named Patrick, who called himself my fairy godmother and loved doing my eyeshadow. But the girls in the club eyed me warily, like they couldn't figure me out.

After months of standing around, unexpectedly, a ginger-headed butch in a leather jacket approached me. She walked tall, with a well-worn swagger, though she wasn't more than a year older than me. She appraised me with a cool glance, tipped her chin up pridefully and said, "Hi. I'm Jodi. Can I buy you a drink?"

She bought me a pineapple juice and we instantly found that we were two nerds with an excitable sense of humor. Her pickup line was, "Do you have 11 protons? Cause you're sodium fine." We got to talking about anime, and she mentioned that she was an artist. An artist? A nerd? GAY? It felt like Persephone herself flung a queer cornucopia of fortune directly into my lap. When Jodi asked if I'd like to see some sketches in her car, I practically flew off of my barstool to follow her out into the night. We casually walked down two alleys in the seediest area of the SOMA to her car.

I sat in her passenger seat as we flipped through her sketchbooks of amateur Hentai. My first thought was, "Oh Jesus, Sailor Mars isn't supposed to be in that position with Cthulu," and then, "She watches Sailor Moon too! This is fate." When she asked me out on a date, I leapt at the opportunity and thought to myself,

I can finally see what lesbian dating is all about. I bet women are so sensitive and intuitive, we will spend the entire night talking about art, getting lost real deep into each other's souls.

She picked me up at my dorm at the University of San Francisco.

"I have a surprise for you-- we're going to The Castro tonight!" Jodi said.

I smiled and watched the lights of the city as we zoomed through the streets. I'd only ever been to The Castro one other time. When I was first questioning my sexuality, I went to the school library, then stupidly typed into a research box: "Am I gay?" and found several resources in the city to check out, one of them being a gay bookstore in The Castro. Every other lesbian I've known has some hot story about losing their virginity to her best friend in high school or college when they discovered themselves, and perhaps afterwards they snuggled under a delightful, rainbow quilt of cats. Not me-- I used the Dewey Decimal System.

Jodi's car rolled to a stop. I thought maybe we'd walk over to a cafe across the street, get peanut butter hot chocolates and talk about *Final Fantasy VII*. She led me by the hand as we passed by tall, good-looking men in leather, assless chaps.

"Ah! Here we are!" she said, pulling around the corner.

It wasn't the cafe. Instead, Jodi had driven me to the nearest sex toy shop. I didn't know a G-D thing about sex toys. I didn't even own a bullet vibrator, or one of those little feather riding crops that newbies like to rock at the Folsom Street Fair. Everywhere I looked, there were ball gags and cock rings. I spun around nervously and accidentally knocked over several bottles of peach flavoured lube. At this point, I was a virgin who kissed one boy a grand total of two times and was now being asked by my lesbian date if she could come in through the VIP entrance or the service door.

"Um...I think it's a bit soon to be talking about dildos, don't you? Wouldn't you like to go out for a coffee and talk, or maybe grab a slice at Nizarios?"

"I don't know, I kind of just wanted to get laid," she sighed.

Jodi put the ten incher and the shocker back on the shelf.

I felt relieved I wouldn't have to attempt either on this monumental evening.

"Let me take you home. I'm sorry this didn't work out, but I'd really like to be friends," she said.

Two seasons of waiting around at Faith had culminated in approximately five minutes of shopping for unwanted butt plugs with a stranger. I'd hoped for so much more. And by more, I didn't mean length OR girth. Maybe, I thought, we'd spend more time together and form some kind of a romantic connection. I was desperate to feel close to someone romantically. At 19, I felt like the Methuselah of virgins.

Sometimes in present-day New York, I see a really run-down bodega with a litany of health code violations, a sign defiantly hanging in the window that says something like, "TRY THE WORLD'S BEST SANDWICHES!" in 575-point, bold red Helvetica font. If that bodega were a person, it would be me attempting to get laid before I hit 20. You need that kind of chutzpah to make it in Manhattan—looking back, I don't know how I had that kind of confidence coming out on my own at 19. Somehow, going to bars and flirting with strangers seemed to be the most direct approach to getting what I wanted. Yet I hadn't expected it to be so unfulfilling.

As we drove back to campus, I glanced out of the window and wondered what I had gone wrong. "Don't look so sad," Jodi said. "Listen, I'm starting a henna tattoo business, maybe I can come over next weekend and give you one on your arm? It'll only last a week or two."

I hopped out of Jodi's car and went back into my dorm. My roommate looked up from her books. "Home already? That was fast," she said. I burst into sobs as she gently patted my back and we went out for a strawberry sundae. Most of the other students were out drinking, and while I certainly could have used two or three drinks of anything at that point, drinking and drugs were something I feared experimenting with at that age. Half Filipino and half German, I've always had a strange mix of first and third world personal values. I'd never shielded myself away from wild social taboos, like getting a VCH piercing, but I also would never have fathomed breaking the actual law by drinking two years before the age of 21. My family grew up under the reign of Marcos, and I was raised with a fear and reverence of the authorities.

Although the night ended in disappointment, it only took me a day or two to shake it off-- I was determined and recommitted myself to make another pilgrimage to Faith, next Thursday.

Faith was part of a larger club, City Nights. Each night of the week had a rotating theme, and Faith, the only gay night, ran on a Thursday. I found out about it when I accidentally got dragged to City Nights by the other girls in my dorm for, "Ladies Night." It turned out to be a hetero party featuring male strippers. One of my friends ended up falling for a fireman that leaped off the stage; he undulated at her and tied a cherry from the bar into a knot with his tongue.

I danced a little with an old bald guy who was a dead ringer for Moby, zoning out, secretly wishing he were a woman, and wanting to leave. When the time came for us to head back to the dorms, I went to grab my coat at the check and saw a flyer for Faith on the floor. I picked it up and slipped it into my pocket, making the decision to go on my own to the gay night in secret next week.

One-part gritty warehouse and one-part industrial BDSM rave decor, Faith was the only place in all of Northern California where someone my age could find community or a mate. It started out in a small bar in Walnut Creek and after losing the venue, built up a devoted following of young, thirsty, underaged club kids in San Francisco. The only way to get in was by somehow getting on a rather obscure guest list through a friend of a friend or someone working at the bar. If not, you'd wait in a line wrapping around the entire block and be turned away as soon as it filled to capacity within an hour. The combination of getting on an email list when not many people went online, knowing the staff from going so often, and unexpectedly later working at the bar as a dancer meant, thankfully, that I never got turned away from Faith when I needed it the most.

Faith had a shy and youthful optimism about it, no one there was generally older than 20. We were the JV party crew of the day and once our peers turned 21, they hit the Castro circuit, never to be seen again. A crowd of partygoers decked in purple fauxhawks, feather boas, vinyl pants and black nail polish came from as far as three hours away to find themselves. We hadn't grown old enough yet to know the slings and arrows of cruising gay bars, or to see scores of friends or lovers devastated by substance abuse. We were young and excited to meet other people on the dance floor to songs like Amber's, "This is Your Night." Since nobody was old enough to even buy a beer, the most sinful way we ended our nights was by eating disco fries at Denny's at 2am. Still, I wasn't totally sheltered at Faith. Every now and then, I'd see someone sneak in an airplane-sized bottle of vodka, or occasionally pop a brightly colored pill that looked like a Lucky Charm on their tongue.

On those early nights, I felt a deep loneliness, watching waves of strobes and lasers flicker and consume the crowd, their sweat mixing with glitter. I had no queer mentors, apart from Jodi, who was now my wing woman (and she got laid almost every time we went out). One particularly depressing night, I sat there quietly drinking another pineapple juice and analyzing my life. I'd lost most of my friends, who were practicing "Christians" that I used to study with at our Christian High School. They seem to call less since I started exploring my sexuality, it was clear they weren't exactly enthusiastic about my "lifestyle choice."

I'd moved to the city from Stockton, CA, forever immortalized as one of the poorest farm towns in the state; a land amalgamated of meth, asparagus crops and born-again hillbillies. I didn't have friends other than my roommate, with whom I quickly shared an instant compatibility over Alice Deejay, Pre-Raphaelite paintings, and Cheez-Its. Back then, I'd tried to hold onto my belief in God, but after getting kicked out from my prayer group, it became clear I had to leave behind my old life and keep pressing forward even if it seemed daunting. Growing up half-Filipino and half-German, I was used to not fitting in or meeting people who shared my cultural values. But coming out on my own felt like I was alone on an entirely new level.

Faith was what I needed. At the club I knew I was a part of something greater, even on the nights when I left the club solo and listening to Alice Deejay on my Discman in a taxi on the way home at 2am.

Six months after my first date with Jodi, I was at Faith yet again. I'd left behind a Christian High School, lost religious friends and family members as I started to slowly tell people that I thought I might be gay. As the list of people in my life grew smaller, I felt lonelier than ever hanging out at this bar. Suddenly, a House song with heavy, seductive bass came on. Frankie Knuckles once called House music, "Church for people who've fallen from grace." Something about this song lit me up. I began bouncing to the beat, listening for a synthesized organ sample that made me think of the Wednesday night prayer group I'd left behind.

Suddenly, I locked eyes with a dark-haired, femme raver across the dancefloor, her lashes lined heavily with Urban Decay sparkles. Nervous, I looked away. I looked back and she smiled, then walked over. I'd seen her before with the other girls at the club, and I was drawn to her the first time I saw her. Since she'd never said a word in all this time, I thought she simply wasn't interested and had been too shy myself to find out.

"So the other girls don't know what to make of you," she said, with an easy grin.

"Oh?"

"Yeah, we see you walk in here by yourself every week. What's your story? Are you gay or just looking for someone for your boyfriend?"

Irritated, I turned from her.

"I'm gay," I said, annoyed that after all I'd done to prove myself; it still wasn't enough.

"How many women have you been with?"

"Well, none," I muttered.

"How can you know you're gay if you've never been with a woman?" she said, throwing up her hands.

"Well I don't have any interest in men. I thought that might be a major indicator." I said.

I felt in that moment she was making a fool of me, that maybe coming to Faith every week was a mistake. I looked for an exit. Before I could storm out, she grabbed me by my candy bead necklace, each one blossoming bright electroshock pops of orange and cyan in the dark, lighting up the wilds of her eyes.

"This necklace looks nice on you," she said, pulling me in closer with her fingertip.

"It's yours now!"

I took it off with zero hesitation and placed it around her neck.

She laughed lightly, somewhat delighted at the effortless power she had over me.

"I won't let you leave tonight, without knowing," she whispered.

She pulled me in and gave me a gentle kiss, sparks of white-hot pain shot through me as she bit my lip. I felt the primal neon halo of all the stars in the cosmos touch deep within my chest, pounding. The only guy I'd ever kissed was my high school boyfriend. I'd known him since we were twelve and the kiss felt empty and wrong.

When this gorgeous stranger kissed me, I felt like I'd been lost for so long and was finally coming home to something. After that moment, I'd never again be afraid to walk into a gay bar, war with religious family members, be called a dyke, or talk to strangers in The Castro and The Village and make friends with other people who seemed just as lonely. Her kiss branded within me a gentle courage, her lips measured against the weight of my heart and found the depths of it unyielding.

That kiss marked me, revealed my deepest truth and changed my entire life. And that was all it took to let me know that maybe Faith, with its $5 pineapple juices and my fellowship of punk rock 18-year-old drag queens from Fresno, was exactly what I needed after all.

Peaches in the City of Sodom

Río Alvia

Coming out was the beginning of this sacramental life.
Every word I use is a sacrilegious song to rectify Leviticus- The
passages I fear most on Sunday mornings.
I was taught there are no peaches in the city of Sodom.
We sang hymns of its supposed truth.
But I am contrasting colors, a programmed Christian that
learned to run.
Far enough to understand my worth.
I am delectability queer like ripen peaches in the early spring.
Sweet as self-love born out my queerness, cultivated from small
acts of visibility.
Creating a home out of kindred strangers that made space for
me in ways my family never could.
Affirmation, a love language in native tongues never taught to
us as children.
Still, I birthed jubilee out of the years in silence and rug burned
knees from repenting my greatest sin.
It wasn't my greatest sin, but the resurrection of me.
Who I was through this process only sweetened the fruit.
My taste remains dulce like the mana I prayed so long for.

The promised land is June 2013 in kaleidoscope colors spilling
through Greenwich.
Christened on the streets blessed by Marsha P Johnson and the
brick that brought me providence in queer liberty.
Baptised by arms of those who love in the ways that I do.
The streets trembled as the confluent laughter and glee
overthrew all of New York City.
I found myself at the center of the place rebuked during our
sermons.

Learning my indoctrination was falsified.
Peaches grow in any season, winter fruit having the hardest
journeys but the sweetest juice.
There was power in queerness and joy in outness, to peel back
the skin that never was you.
Breathe in new air.
In this truth one could be radically queer and soft as the fuzz on
the skins of disallowed fruits in Eden.

In my youth falling in love was the first instance of
understanding what it meant to be overtaken by el espíritu.
Whispering forbidden lovers' names into prayer.
Unfriending best friends that sing your heart into sapphic red.
Taking chances at the top of the Ferris wheel.
El sabor de verano on lovers' lips and the paradox that was her
tongue wrapped around mine.
There is no finer God than women.
Eternal was the nectar between her thighs, redefining holy spirit
for orgasm.

Queerness is religion.
I am faultlessly me- ripen peach thriving in the city I was taught
to fear.
Exalting this identity, living outside the binary.
Praising this very temple while rejoicing in who I truly am.
Sodom the place where the fruits grow when ready and never
seasonally.
I found home-
this city is my joy.

A Road
(Not Otherwise
Specified)

Sara Sugar-Anyanwu

He told me on the phone, "I've been seeing someone." I felt an already-hollow place in my chest widen. "We've been dating a few months. You'll meet her when you come visit."

I pulled my 1999 blue Volkswagen off the road, parked on a narrow shoulder of the Pacific Coast Highway and left the keys dangling in the ignition. I didn't know what to say. It felt like air was being sucked out of my lungs and my insides were collapsing.

"I mean, if you want." That's what my on-and-off boyfriend of nearly five years said. We can call him Jake.

No! I don't fucking want to meet her, I wanted to scream. But I didn't say that. Instead, I turned off the engine and sat, staring out over the dashboard of the car towards the teal waters of the Pacific Ocean.

The California sun was starting to heat up the inside of the car and the backsides of my thighs were sweating, sticking grossly to the seat. I don't remember what I said to him next—I must have at least said goodbye—though it would have been characteristic of me back then to just hang up. What I do remember is sitting on the side of the road, just steps from the ocean, thinking about how another vehicle could easily skid off the road and hit my car, instantly killing, or worse, paralyzing me. I thought about how I could be pushed into the ocean and drowned in the front seat of the car. Both of these options seemed easier than facing the truth, that without Jake as my beard I was forced to confront the one part of me that I'd dodged for years, being gay.

. . .

I used to joke that when I discovered I was gay;
I didn't come out of the closet but out. As if it was
just that easy. Like one of those cartoon lightbulbs
went on in my brain and then the rest of me—heart
and body—just fell into step. But over the years, I've
learned something simple: The older you get, and the
more hindsight you're allotted, the more you discover
that your younger self was really just full of shit.

After 15 years of living life as an out queer woman,
I now know who I am. I'm gay. I no longer end this
statement with a question mark, denoting uncertainty,
but with the definitive punctuation of a period. Half
a dozen years ago, my father looked at me and good
humoredly said, "You're the gayest person I know." I
took pride in that. Not because he knows lots of gay
people, he doesn't, but because I really like being gay.
I like the community: the bars, the drag shows, the
sweaty Pride dance parties, how if you're in a crowd
of queers it doesn't matter who you are, because you
just belong. I like the lesbian ensemble: the blazers, the
wingtips, the hoodies, the no-makeup makeup (or just
no makeup). And of course, I like the women.

But I wasn't always like this.

I was pruned to be an anorexic, heterosexual figure
skater, assumed to marry the boy next door. I laugh
at this now. My curvy, queer, lady-loving-self chuckles
and shakes her head as she writes this. Not because
my story of coming out was easy, or fun, or quick, or

should be trivialized, but because I know how my story turns out.

I knew I was gay, or at least not straight, from a young age. How young? I'm not sure. But what I do know is that at some point, I made an unconscious decision to bury this fact. The athlete in me knows that if you practice something long enough, you can get good at most things. And if you're good at something, good at being something, it's easier to convince yourself that that's how you're supposed to be. And I did: I practiced. I rehearsed being straight—with the clothes, boyfriends, and the gossip. Being someone else wasn't really that hard; TV, glossy magazines and growing up in waspy Connecticut made it easier than maybe it should have been.

Figure skating also allowed a superb camouflage. Despite the outward-facing beauty of the sport, skating was a toxic environment, where my body was trained to conform to exhausting standards. My 5'7" frame—towering over most women on ice—was critiqued and whittled down to a more manageable form. I quickly learned what size my body needed to be for me to deserve love. I also learned that that love should come from a man.

One of my coaches, let's call her Ukrainian Barbie, liked to comment a lot on my appearance. She was two inches taller than me, sported breasts settling seamlessly into a D-cups, and took a smaller pant size than me. She liked to remind me often of that last fact a lot. As the weight on the scale dropped, she'd say things like, "You're a great advertisement for me!" Or, "You were meat and milk before I started with you." My body eventually became acceptable to her, but never quite perfect. It was always a shame that my breasts got so small or that my thighs didn't go straight up and down. In a way, I supposed I was her life-sized Barbie. She told me how to dress, when to change my shoes, and gave me her hand-me-down clothes. She once handed me a bronze lace dress. "It's from Greece," she said in her thick accent. "I think you will finally fit into it."

Figure skating was familial and beatific, yet dysfunctional. It was an idyllic-looking family from the outside, one with glowing parents and unsoiled children, where boys wore neckties and girls ribbons. But under the surface there was an abscess, where noxious words and verbal abuse festered.

. . .

When I entered high school, it was easy to pass. The boy next door and I dated five years spanning into my freshman year of college. But still, I tip-toed around the borders of my sexual feelings; kissing a few girls here, going further with a few there. I never let myself marinate too long on the idea that I could be gay. Instead, I leaned into the Girls Gone Wild trope, the girls that kiss other girls to makes boys holler, or the the ones that watch lesbian porn with their boyfriends. It wasn't that black and white, but it was easier to pretend it was.

As high school stretched on, my disordered eating blossomed into a full-fledged eating disorder. I'd eat, I wouldn't eat, I'd lose weight, I'd gain weight. I saw a therapist, then a nutritionist, then another therapist.

Then I got depressed. But maybe I was depressed first and then my eating disorder exploded. Maybe I started to suspect that I wasn't straight and that caused me to fuck more with my eating. Which came first, the chicken or the egg? I don't think I'll ever know.

People like to label things: anorexia, bulimia, eating disorder NOS (Not Otherwise Specified)—it's our human nature to want to classify and categorize—to check boxes: straight, gay, bisexual. We like the ability to place our chattels in order, to map them out. First this happened, then this, then this. It provides us with a sense of control to know what came first and second. Because then maybe we'll be able to predict what comes next. I'll admit, when all actions and events are said and done, it does make it easier to tell a story. But in looking at my life honestly, I know there are many things I'll never be able to put properly in place.

People also like to say that, "things just spiraled!" when telling a story where the outcome is less than gratifying. I've always liked how this sounded, it's neat and tidy. If you're going to hit rock bottom, you might as well just go for it in one fell swoop. But getting to rock bottom for me took some time. There were ups and downs, ER visits, in-patient stays, so much weight—both gained and lost—before I bottomed out.

After four tumultuous years of high school I took a year off to figure skate, get my head on straight and let overzealous psychiatrists put me on every psychotropic medication they had in their arsenal. I was put on the ones that make you happy, the ones that calm you down, then the ones that are supposed to counteract the negative side effects of the previous ones. I saw a therapist, and a psychiatrist, a nutritionist, and then another psychiatrist, and on and on. Regardless of where they came in the lineup, they all had one common goal: They tried to make me whole. But all the meds and talking were just Band-Aids. The following fall, despite everyone's best efforts, I headed off to college in fragmented pieces.

. . .

I went to college to skate, to learn how to be a world class coach. I dreamt of going to the Olympics, not as a competitor but as one of those stern looking coaches sitting in the kiss and cry. It probably goes without saying, but I never got further than watching the melodrama of the Olympics on TV. Because for me, college was where the wrong thing took center stage, not my athleticism or grades, but my eating disorder.

I could have chosen a liberal arts college for writing, where people walk around barefoot, smoke weed and eat potato chips while debating whether or not to stop shaving their pits. Maybe I wouldn't have gotten so sick or maybe I would have come out earlier. But instead, I chose a petri dish of misogyny and heteronormativity. It was the kind of environment where during a group workout at the ice rink a male trainer singled me out for a conversation on whether my butt needed more work or whether it was just unfortunate panty lines. "Maybe you just shouldn't wear underwear," he said. It was that kind of environment. The constant dieting, the working out, the incessant comments about weight, shape, size and muscle tone was normalized by everyone in the skating world—encouraged by coaches, trainers and skaters alike. Being alarmingly thin was glamorized. The most applauded skaters had bodies like rails. And as much as you're supposed to be skeletal, erasing your body of unnecessary curves, you're still supposed to be sexy and alluring. Skating is a dangerous place for women (and men), full of contradictions. It's like holding a person's head underwater, then, while watching them thrash about, screaming at them to take a deep breath.

. . .

Maybe if it had just been the eating disorder, I would have pulled myself up from my skate laces and made it work, maybe I wouldn't have fallen so far. But it wasn't just my eating disorder that was holding me just below that surface, waiting for me to drown, it was the other thing I wasn't ready to face. As much as skating is dangerous for your physical health, it's also a superb closet to hide out in if you think you're gay but not ready to admit it. Because, as long as I still skated, as long as I still dated the boy next door, as long as I wore the clothes, flirted back, then no one would suspect. Skating was a great place to hide.

. . .

Away at school, the pounds started again to rapidly drop (the stopgap that had been put in place during my gap year had been whittled away) and I became one of those skaters whose weight was too low to be allowed on the ice to practice. After winter break, instead of going back to school I boarded a plane bound for Los Angeles and an in-patient treatment facility. Though looking like a bobble head on a dashboard, I still saw myself as too large. "It's body dysmorphia," they said. But I didn't understand how that could be when I could feel myself warm and heavy with flesh. I would lie awake at night daydreaming of zipping off long swaths of fat from myself to reveal a cool, crisp, angular version. I was never able to let myself see what was truly reflected in the mirror, and that included not letting myself see a gay woman.

. . .

After Jake called me on the phone that night and broke things off, I drove to the main house of the treatment facility to see my therapist. I'd done well enough in therapy to be able to live a few miles down the road in a transitional facility; think halfway house for women who are still learning to feed themselves. We sat on the wooden porch outside the house.

"Do you know what this means?" I asked her, wailing like a child who'd been told that Santa Claus wasn't real. She nodded. "It means I have to deal with my sexuality!" It meant I had no more excuses. There was no boyfriend left to hide behind, skating had been taken away, there was nothing left. At least nothing that felt like an excuse anymore for not coming out. Finally, that voice in my head that liked to whisper on repeat,

"But I have a boyfriend!" faltered and fell silent.

That night, I tried my new self on for size. *I'm not straight.* I whispered to myself. *I'm gay.* The words settled heavily in my gut. Coming out wasn't going to be fun, I knew that much. I desperately wanted for a shortlist of next steps, best practices for baby gays. Circa early 2000s, there wasn't YouTube or Instagram, no hashtags or threads for me to scroll through and feel enlightened by or connected to. Parents still screamed and disowned their children as they crept out of the closet and timidly looked around. Being gay in my eyes I saw as a sad, second-best thing. I felt at a loss for what to do, so I cried, one of those rib-aching, blood vessel-popping cries, the sort that's typically reserved for death. But for me, this was a death, so many parts of me were dying. I cried for all the things I had been groomed to be and to want, for the little girl who was put on a diet at age 8, and for the teenager whose coach's expectations were always just out of reach. I cried heart-wrenchingly for the young woman who thought that being someone else would be easier and less painful than living her truth. Then, I cried for all the things I thought that I had lost and would never have: a marriage, a family, happiness. The list was achingly long, and I mourned for all of it.

. . .

There are many months around the time when I came out that are foggy—leaving the treatment center and ultimately the West Coast, moving in on my own, starting school again are a blur—but those first few weeks after I decided to come out, first to myself and then others, are crystal clear. I felt something tangible during that time, more real than at any other juncture in my life, like I could pluck the moments from the air, hold them gently in the palm of my hand, turn them over and examine their angles, their composition, what made them feel real.

It took immense courage, but in those weeks I started to explore my sexuality. I was like a sponge, absorbing everything about myself that I could. I had questions and fears, a list that felt endless, and three thousand miles away from home, I felt alone. I leaned on my therapist who was also gay, a few friends I'd make during my stay in treatment and bought a copy of *A Straight Girl's Guide to Sleeping with Chicks*. I also watched a lot of *The L Word* episodes that my therapist taped for me on VHS.

"Just watch it," she said. "See how it makes you feel." So I did, slinking out of my room one night and popping the tape into the VCR. Pushing play, I sat on the floor, crouching tiger, hidden dragon style, ready to pounce and turn it off at the first sound of footsteps.

The L Word—let's be clear, I'm talking about the original, because there is a difference—was softcore porn, basic smut, but my therapist was on to something, I felt things, not just sexual, but also a bruising desire for freedom to live how I wanted. Maybe, I thought, I could be like Carmen and Bette and Alice and all the others in the show (I could even be Shane!). Maybe I could live life as a gay woman and be happy. I was surprised by my appetite. The anticipation gave me goosebumps.

At first, I watched these proud, out women on television alone. But an episode or two in, the skinny butts of my housemates began to fill the couch seats. First came Faith, an olive-skinned Italian girl with dark brown hair that reached nearly to her boney butt. Faith and I used to sit on the Starbucks patio across from Zuma Beach in Malibu and do homework for our respective classes we took at Santa Monica Community College—or SMCC as the locals called it—drink coffee, and celebrity watch. (We saw Minnie Driver once in oversized sunglasses in the parking lot and I very literally bumped into Pamela Anderson once in the grocery store. She was very nice about it.) Faith had an almost never-ending ensemble of Juicy Couture sweatsuits, chained smoked Newports, and spoke with the deep raspy voice of someone 30 years her senior.

"Hey! This is that show," Faith had said, stopping with her evening snack on her way from the kitchen. "The lesbian one?" She was quick to take a seat, folding her willowy limbs underneath her. In the pre-Netflix, pre-streaming days, our TV watching consisted primarily of *Law & Order* episodes, the two of us watched a lot of reruns. *The L Word*, though, was different, novel. At last something new!

My second housemate to trickle in was Julia, tall with fire engine red hair. Barely 19, she was the youngest in the house and joined our TV circle with minimal fanfare. Finally, Vanessa rounded out our viewing party. Older than me, though you'd never have known by her child-sized frame, Vanessa had sandy blonde hair and was distinctly mousey in appearance.

She hung around the periphery for a while, perching on an armrest like a bird, as she often did, before eventually taking a seat.

With these women, I shared not only my coming out, but also this very gay show. Their comradery showed me that I had had it all wrong. I had feared the other girls with me in treatment would freak out about having a not-straight girl in the house, but it was far from the truth. Instead, they were my champions, encouraging me, noticing my growth and being genuinely happy for me. Once at Starbucks, Faith encouraged me to hit on a lady cashier I had always thought was cute. It didn't go so well. I vaguely remember blurting out that I thought she was pretty. Needless to say, I didn't get her number, just a bewildered look.

In our group therapy sessions, I started sharing how I felt about not being straight, opening up about the best friend I'd fallen in love with back in college, our one night of passion, and then her ghosting me. I spoke about my hurt. I spoke about my confusion. I shared how I felt that being gay would be letting down the people I loved. I talked it out, we all talked it out, including how, eventually, I'd come out to my parents.

. . .

Outside the comfort of the treatment facility, my roommates, and the endless parade of therapists and nutritionists through the house, I wasn't sure how else, where else, on who else to practice being my new gay self with. My therapist, always to my rescue, suggested that being around other gay people was a good place to start. So, one afternoon I drove to West Hollywood, turned off the engine and sat in my car. Then I started the car again, drove down another street, parked and sat. I did this on repeat looking for a street that felt less threatening, less intimidating. They never did. I did this for days. Each time, returning to my therapist who would ask, "How did it go?"

It felt paralyzing and pathetic. I wasn't frightened to be pegged as gay, not anymore. I wanted to be seen. I craved community, someone to talk and ask questions to. No, I wasn't scared of being identified as gay anymore, but like an old friend creeping back up on me, I was scared of my appearance and how I looked moving through the world. This time, though, instead of being frightened of my body, of appearing too large or too bulky, I was scared of not fitting in. I felt as if I walked around with "baby lesbian" tattooed on my forehead, not knowing how to act or what to say.

The desire to shed my loneliness and belong eventually won out, and after a lot of internal dialogue with myself, I drove back into West Hollywood, parked and forced myself out of the car. I walked around, head down, in a deer-in-headlights type way. Strolling by The Abbey, the inspiration for a cafe on *The L Word*, I slowed my amble to a crawl and peered through the courtyard. My mind on repeat: I'll be back.

. . .

There were more solo outings after, driving down

Hollywood Boulevard, stopping at the Pacific Design Center, a Buddhist gift shop that smelled of sweet incense and a trip to A Different Light bookstore where I purchased a sexually charged queer book of fairytales. I never read it, but it sits on a bookshelf to this day in our home, flanked by *Tipping the Velvet* and *Three Women*.

The weekend of Los Angeles Pride, I drove again into West Hollywood, this time with Julia as my accomplice, to see Blondie headline the LGBT Pride Festival. I wish I could say I danced hard, giving no fucks, but I didn't. I stood towards the back bopping my head, all the while feeling an overwhelming sense of kinship with those around me. After the music, I got my bellybutton pierced, a gaudy glass rainbow earring protruded from my abdomen. I thought it was the gayest thing ever, it wasn't. I thought I would love how my stomach looked with it in, I didn't. I took it out early the next morning, but I felt pretty badass for those 12 hours.

There was a woman's party at The Abbey but Julia wasn't 21, so we wandered some instead and landed at a googie-esque diner. Being the kickoff of pride, inside it was packed with a rainbow of queers—the loud, the quiet, the coupled, the not. I ordered two eggs sunny side up, wheat toast and sliced tomatoes. I saw and felt how normal it all was: the 24-hour diner, the short order food and, of course, the people. So many people, my people! LGBTQ folks not just living life but celebrating it. I sat and ate my food, all the while wondering if I could ever be that brave.

As we walked back to the car it was late, trash was

being picked up from the curb and the sidewalks were being hosed down. It almost didn't register, but then it did that for the first time in years I'd gone to an all-night diner and eaten more than my allotted three meals and two snacks. The food had been salty, greasy and fucking amazing. Without knowing it, without even really paying attention, I'd turned a corner in my recovery.

That night I uncovered a hunger that wouldn't be satiated by eating too much, too little, or nothing at all. I was still scared of being gay (of course I was), I can't lie and say anything different. I wish I could say that after that night that I came out on the other side, bright-faced, happy and proud, but I can't. There would be many more years of hurt and struggle and pain. But that night, all the drudgery of self-hate, all the bullshit and struggling in my recovery, it all started to feel manageable.

Eventually (very eventually), I do things I've never done before. I grill steak. I enjoy food. I move to New York City. I date women. I wear a bathing suit. I finish school. I fall madly in love. I get married. All in that exact order.

. . .

It's 15 years later from the time I sat on the dusty elbow of the Pacific Coast Highway. It's the last call for pictures. The photographer comes to my wife and I and asks if there are any last images he wants us to take, to preserve indefinitely. It's our wedding. It's perfect. Looking out across the East River towards Manhattan, we're tipsy on booze and love, all the things you're supposed to be. But without a moment's hesitation, we know that there is one last photo we need. We turn to our queer family—some buzzed, some sloppy drunk, all wide with smiles—and wave them over. They are the picture we need; men, women, young, old, queer, gay, bi, nearly all the letters under the umbrella. My sister joins—she's one of us.

We congregate in a haphazard semi-circle, so much strength, so many stories. The photo could represent me finally being ok with who I am (or an advertisement for an "It gets better" campaign), but it's so much more. It's not just me, or my journey. Instead, it's a caravan of travelers, each with their own unique itinerary of strength and love and perseverance, all converging at a single moment to celebrate a milestone that's still very new to our community, but so precious. We smile at the camera, sweaty, glowing—I'm overwhelmed by a sense of belonging—and on the count of three, we all scream: "Family!"

Boundaried Love

Maria Garcia

I had been here before, ready to say it all, about to say it all if just pushed a bit more. I wanted her to know how I was feeling, what I was feeling. I felt like I had fallen victim to the classic patient-therapist trope where the patient falls for the therapist leaving the patient on an emotional rollercoaster. Why, I thought, would I spend my money on telling my therapist I was having fantasies about her? Obsessing over her profile on *Psychology Today*, googling her name and zooming into her pictures; inch by inch not knowing what I was looking to find; the time on her wrist, the liquid in her cup, the shade of lipstick on her smile.

Every time I thought it was important to bring up my feelings, something more urgent would arise and I'd put it on the shelf for another day. One day, I thought, I would take it out, open it and with the casualness of speaking about the weather, and confess this love I have for her. With the passing of time the intensity would be gone, becoming a light comment, almost like a joke. We would then both tilt our heads back in laughter while reaching out for our calendars to schedule our next session.

Just as I was trying to think of anything else, other than my obsession to talk about, the bangles on her wrist broke the silence we had been maintaining. The sound reminded me of how present she was, not only in our shared physical space but in my actual life, rattling around in the background like her bracelets. For somebody like her, who sits comfortably in silence for a living, it was probably easy. But for me, it felt like a constant challenge. My impulse was to fill the air with chatter and question her about mundane observations regarding her choice of plants in her tiny office and the books lining her shelf.

I liked looking at her soft brown hair, highlighted by the ray of sun sneaking through the window, the life lived showing under her eyes, her small body, and her hands holding her crossed knee. I liked how her hands were veiny, but strong with short nails. Her thin lips and her fine nose always poking at me. I liked looking at her, although not straight to the eyes, that felt threatening.

"Your eyebrows!" I said louder than expected with a gasp breaking the silence. Her calm monotone expression transformed into a wide-eyed look while her body shuffled around in her chair.

"What about them?" she asked.

"They look different," I said hesitantly. "Thicker with more color." I wasn't sure if it made her look more attractive or more like a stranger. Eyebrows are everything. Take somebody's eyebrows out and good luck. I remembered those thin eyebrows that were misshapen during our teenage years in 2005, half oval like, which now have a hard time growing back. I like thick, big eyebrows the caterpillar type. But since I'd met her, I didn't recall her eyebrows having that shape and color.

Jaime left her knee unattended, quickly touching her left eyebrow. I knew this was more of an unplanned, human response than a therapist response. She should have continued to stare at me and ask me questions. I was testing her all the time to prove to me that she was in fact a human.

After the eyebrow interruption, she caught onto

my act of avoidance and played her best card: silence. She waited for me to tell her what had been on my mind since I left her the week before. My partner and I had gone to the movies to see *Carol*, a love story between a young woman and a married woman in the 1950's.

Only a few times in my life have I felt a force beyond my control gluing me to the seat, opening my eyes while transporting me so deep into the story that I am unable to come back. For reasons unknown to me this film was one of them. After that day, the only thing I did was cry, replaying the movie in my mind. This overwhelming feeling of emotions rushed through, bursting open the doors of my consciousness and tearing apart my rational thoughts. The result was streams of tears that melted away in the hot water of my bathtub where I spent countless hours revisiting the film's scenes; the glances interchanged, the delicate hands; on each other's bodies, wrapped around the martini glass, holding the cigarettes, closing the doors, words exchanged as they opened their lives to one another.

I bought the book, *The Price of Salt*, that the movie was based on and I devoured it in one sitting. The book and movie made me realize I was Therese (Rooney Mara) in the film and that there had been many Carols (Cate Amazing Blanchett) in my life. Since I can remember I have always had female role models who I admired so deeply that I would think of them every night before going to bed and every morning when I woke up. Although the relationship mostly felt like a one-way street, they all surprised me by allowing a deeper access into their world.

My third-grade teacher asked my parents if I could come to her house and bake a cake. I remember her helping me finish my homework in her childhood bedroom where she still lived before heading downstairs to have dinner. The cake we had made earlier was waiting on the counter to be cut. The chocolate frosting softened on my plate while I tried to eat it properly.

"Do you like it?" she asked as she was finishing her piece, delicately licking her fork "You can take the rest home," she said as she stood up, the anxiety of the "the end" approaching, hitting my stomach who was occupied digesting a sugar rush.

A few years later, my dance teacher asked me to come with her and pick up our dance recital costumes, driving around her Sentra while we discussed the other girls in the classroom, sharing information that I knew she had to trust me to do so; somebody's parent being overly involved in the recital, a close friend of mine not being the dancer she thought she was, the secretary at our dance school wasting too much time listening to our stories filled with childlike fantasies, making her slow at her job. The sense of responsibility of this information weighed on my shoulders, alleviated by the wind coming into the front seat, caressing my hair pulled back on a perfect ballerina bun.

"Your tenacity," she added, as if to close her train of thought, "will take you further than you can imagine." When I got home that night I ran upstairs, forgetting to greet my parents, closing the door behind me, frantically dusting off the dictionary my aunt had given me years prior which had only been looked at once, when my back was hurting and in wanting to be specific in describing my pain I found the word "scapula" and used it in a sentence that left everyone impressed at the doctor's office.

"Tenacity," I hadn't stopped repeating the word, dissecting it, multiplying it, memorizing it since she had mentioned it. I did not want to forget it, this way I would discover what she meant, what she thought of me, about my character, the way I conducted myself in this world. As I finished reading the definition, I closed the book, swinged it in the air as I fell on my back in my twin bed, eyes and mouth wide open, gasping for air as one does after climaxing. It was the best day of my life.

"Paint your nails so they look pretty while you help her grade papers," my mom said knowing I was spending too much time with my high school literature teacher. My family knew about these women and the role they played in my life.

. . .

"How are your 'obsessions' today?" my brother used to tease me. How is it, I thought, that he knows? Sitting down in front of him at the kitchen table I became hyper aware of every move I was making. Did I look happier? Did I say their name too much? As he devoured his plate of food, I chewed carefully, my secrets were coming out and I wanted to contain them in a tight, corroded Mason Jar.

"You collect women," my college professor said

to me while we sat inside her car outside the English building. She often drove me to my dorm after classes taking short detours where we shared ideas about constructed culture and I wrestled my constant impulse of touching her leg. She knew some of my stories regarding these obsessions through an essay I had written and had shared with her. The writing described my love for these women in my life, wishing she had found herself identified with the rest of them therefore knowing how special she was to me. The statement caught me off guard, had she misunderstood my words and actions, that instead of feeling special, she had been feeling like she was just like the rest? It was the first time I realized I did in fact collect these strong sexless relationships where I knew I was the most special person to the woman of the moment, and she was the most special to me.

Having experienced these multiple times, I knew the process. I would meet somebody who happened to be in some sort of an authoritative role, something about them would spark intense interest in me and I would get very close to them. It never failed and they all let me in. It was as if they too found something in me, an attention that perhaps they had been missing as well and that somehow, my young self was filling. From gifts given to me which became like trophies to long car rides with all these Carols, I believe to have been falling in love with women my whole life. I didn't know it then, but the thrill of being in the car with her, baking cakes with her, grading papers and watching her hair blow in the wind was opening the door to their magical world. I was enamored. Jaime, my therapist, nodded and maintained eye contact while I finished telling her about Carol through uncontrolled sobs. It was as if the movie had brought me back to every single one of these relationships and I realized for the first time in my life how much heartbreak I had been carrying.

Being in therapy with a blondish therapist (like Carol) while I had my own darker hair and younger age (like Therese) did not help. Was this my subconscious opening the floodgates to all my desires: past and future that were crashing together? Was it the longing of all of my "collection of women" ending with moving in together permanently? The reality was that none of them had ended up like that. These were teachers and married women with their own lives; not to mention it would have been unethical for them to be entangled with me, but now here was another Carol giving me an alternative reality of what these older women and I could have done.

Instead of moving in together or confessing our love to one another, I said goodbye to each and every one of them, when school was over, when I moved away, or when life happened leaving me with a lifetime's worth of unprocessed heartbreaks. Now here I was all these years later trying to understand their impact in my life. My therapist, being the curious being that she was, started asking me questions. For some questions, I had some answers, for others I didn't, and I still don't.

"What do you think Carol represents in your life?" Jaime would put her hands together, forming a diamond shape that she would then raise to her lips, as if she was trying to capture my spoken words. I would then match her expression by resting my face on my hand, covering my lips, as if to tighten the words that were trying to fall out. "I don't know, my mother?" I said thinking of Oedipus, knowingly that that was not how I felt and so did she, giving me in return a frowning face.

She tried again, "What lingering feelings did the movie leave you with? That feeling of grief you described earlier, is it that of the grief of falling in love?" She sighed waiting for my response and the bangles moved, giving my unspoken words a touch of symphony.

I love deeply, I thought. I started to speak in a quiet, gentle voice, almost alien to my usual, louder tone, until I recognized it and was unable to stop.

"I love so intensely, with so many women, including you," I said, gazing at my shoes contrasting the old wooden floor, unable to look Jaime in the eyes. I waited for a quarter of a second to suppress my panic, almost avoiding what her reaction would be. The pressure in my throat had dropped to my stomach, leaving the rest of my body ringing. She knows these confessions very well, I assured myself.

Jaime's hazelnut eyes softened as she leaned forward separating her hands from being together as if she was about to say something important. But she didn't speak. When I finally looked up to meet her gaze, I saw a familiar expression; of love, of tenderness, perhaps sympathy, not pity. Her lips formed a slight smile that embraced my petrified self, holding me in a way I had never experienced before. The silence filled the room and for the first time there was no need for me to fill it. For the first time, I didn't reach for a book or new plant or the weather to occupy the quiet space. In the silence I processed the words, the thoughts and feelings.

I haven't been able to watch *Carol* since that time at the theater and I don't think I'll try again anytime soon. I have instead kept with me my own version of Carol, thinking about the women from my past and the ones that will continue to enter my life, allowing them to captivate me in a unique way, submerging myself in their teachings, in their hypnotizing way of living life, making even the most mundane acts the most intriguing.

I know there will be more Carols to come. I don't know who or how or when, but when I see her, I will recognize her; and just like that our worlds will experience the excitement of a unique existence, that of a love that can't be named, nor tamed, nor shelved. It will linger in the sweetness of frosting, in the air coming in through a window caressing one's cheek, the impulse of touch but yet, with boundaried love.

Not All Lesbians are White: The Suffering and Survival of a Queer South Asian Woman

Alyy Patel

A half dozen of my unused suicide notes from the past lay scattered in front of my eyes, some more crumpled than others. I wrote them when I was almost certain it was the end of my time in this world.

The earliest note was dated to when I was in the seventh grade—the first time I felt an enigmatic attraction to another woman, but lacked the vocabulary in my mother tongue, Gujarati[1], to conceptualize it as *queer*. This feeling was accompanied by a profound sense of defectiveness and loneliness, which remain a malignant plague in my soul. The latest was dated to the final year of my Master's—after nearly a decade of my *queer family* and *blood family* attempting to shed integral aspects of my multifaceted identity. Perhaps reading the notes would allow me to see that I overcame my struggles—or so I thought. I carefully read each note, searching for a sign, any indication that things were getting better. I needed a reminder of why I had been holding onto hope with such a tight grip. As I examined the notes, a theme illuminated, never before fully appreciated: *the unbearable pain of being a queer South Asian womxn.*

For years, I felt as though experiencing joy and ease in loving myself was far beyond my reach. I learned *rejection*, *resistance*, and *resilience* for my intersecting identities before I understood what it meant to be a queer South Asian womxn.

---

[1] Gujarati people are a South Asian ethnic subgroup.

PART I: GRIEF

Exile from South Asian Culture

In order to protect my safety, I felt forced to repress my sexuality before I could fully comprehend it. Although I never heard my family utter queerphobic remarks while growing up, I knew there would be consequences if my parents found out that I was anything but *sanskaari*. My parents have always used the term "sanskaari" in reference to a cookie-cutter life path that I was required to follow as a Desi diasporic daughter: get straight A's in school, work a 9-5 job, marry a "nice Indian boy," buy a suburban home, and have kids. Ma always emphasized that there was no room for screwing up, because "everyone" always had their eyes on me, just waiting for me to mess up somehow—partying, pre-marital dating, or virtually anything gossip-worthy. In senior year of high school, I pushed my luck, hoping that "everyone" referred to "everyone I didn't block on social media." Unfortunately, I wasn't as low-key as I thought. A distant cousin saw my post disclosing my sexuality on a closed Facebook group within my University; she informed her parent, who called my Ma to ask "Is Sonali a lesbian?" Confused and offended, Ma denied the possibility and defensively demanded that Auntie stop spreading such rumours. Soon after, Ma angrily charged into my room to inquire about how and why Auntie asked about my sexual orientation. My heart dropped to the pit of my stomach. I was horrified. I made concerted efforts to appear calm and collected to avoid conveying guilt, as confirming my queerness would risk my psychological safety. I instinctually responded that my LGBTQ+ advocacy posts online may have been misinterpreted, adding that my interest in doing so was rooted in support for my gay best friend, as Ma knew about his sexuality and loved him anyway. Ma paused, glaring suspiciously at me before silently walking away. This was the death bed of our— once strong—relationship as mother and daughter. This game of broken telephone in 2014 marked the onset of substantial queerphobic emotional abuse, which has since escalated in severity.

To this day, I am constantly told that I am selfish for "choosing to dishonour the family name" by "pursuing a gay lifestyle."

To this day, I am regularly emotionally blackmailed with remarks such as "I have given you everything I have, how could you do this to me? You are shameful."

To this day, my blood kin tell me they love me while attempting to manipulate me into rejecting my queer identity. The emotional abuse made me feel as if I was not "Brown enough" because I am queer; as a result, I became emotionally unattached from my South Asian identity.

Exile from LGBTQ+ Culture

I was thrilled to begin exploring the Toronto LGBTQ+ scene in my first year of university, as my previous years were spent sheltered in a conservative white town with limited exposure to queer life. I naïvely believed that the LGBTQ+ community would offer refuge for someone like me—a Brown-skinned womxn with femme-interpreted features. My hopes of being understood and feeling a sense of belongingness in the LGBTQ+ community—which relentlessly and falsely claims to be diverse and inclusive—were shattered too quickly.

I frequented queer spaces, such as Pride events and gay bars, in search of community. Instead, I felt alienated and invisible in a room full of white queers, who had pre-conceived beliefs about my sexuality based on my appearance. Integral aspects of my South Asian identity, such as my long hair, were reinterpreted as manifestations of femininity; this reduced me to heterosexuality in their colonial eyes.

One of the first few times that I frequented a gay bar in Toronto's Gay Village, a white butch woman unprovokedly shouted "straight girls like you need to go back to your straight bars" at me. This painfully uncomfortable experience wasn't isolated. On several occasions, I have explicitly been asked "are you straight?" by drag queens on stage. As someone who unapologetically occupies spaces, I was shocked to find myself feeling deeply uncomfortable by misinterpretations of who I am. I had an inkling that my experiences felt unsettling because I was the only Asian woman in the bar and the only patron singled out for sexually invalidating questions.

My experiences on dating apps confirmed that I'm reduced to heterosexuality because I am a South Asian womxn and the vast majority of white queers are racially ignorant xenophobes. I frequently received microaggressive messages that discredited my sexuality, such as "are you here [on this app] until you get an arranged marriage?" or "have you been with a woman before?" Receiving racial microaggressions as a pick-up line convinced me that shedding my South Asian identity was required in order to be queerly, romantically loved. There was no way for me to know otherwise, as queer South Asian womxn haven't been represented in mainstream LGBTQ+ media, literature, nor spaces. This is how I got stuck in a year-long romantic relationship with a racist white woman, who regularly expressed her disgust and contempt for my South Asian culture. It felt as though every minor stride I made towards sculpting my identity was met with violent blows to the foundation of my existence.

The hegemonic whiteness of queer culture was suffocating and traumatizing. I was required to assimilate to white lesbian norms and aesthetics in order to be seen as validly queer. The failure to do so meant being treated like an outsider by LGBTQ+ community, who refused to acknowledge my queerness insofar as I displayed South Asian traits. However, submitting to colonial queer scripts was an impossible reality for me, as I was required to balance the culturally conflicting expectations of queer identity expression and disclosure demanded by LGBTQ+ and South Asian communities.

My repeated experiences of racial rejection made me resentful of the LGBTQ+ community.

Grieving My Authentic Self

My journey of identity formation was never about

self-discovery, but rather, it was about mastering the art of shifting between different versions of myself in order to protect my safety in each environment. This constant alteration of self was necessary, albeit the cause of my perpetual misery and chronic stress. I was transitioning between performing different versions of myself so often that I navigated life as an actor while watching my authentic sense of self dissipate in front of my eyes. There is no sense of self when you constantly have to mould and adapt; there is no fixed identity when your sense of self is the consistent product of environment—disposed when it's no longer needed, recreated when it is.

My days were spent grieving my sense of belongingness in LGBTQ+ and South Asian communities, as I was exiled from both. I felt forced to choose between abandoning one of my identities; however, doing so would be at the cost of my safety. I was angry and frustrated—it felt as though I was being pulled by opposing forces wanting me to be one without the other.

PART II: RAGE

For several years, I felt resentment towards my South Asian family for subjecting me to queerphobic violence. I was unable to find forgiveness in my heart until I learned that my family's attempts to repress my queerness is a by-product of Britain's sexual civilizing mission in South Asia during the colonial era. My ancestors were once free to engage in queerness without fear of societal judgment, as fluid gender and sexuality was considered normal in pre-colonial South Asia. However, British colonizers perceived our sexual and gender fluidity as "uncivilized" and "barbaric" and thus, violently erased queerness from South Asian culture and history. Situating my experiences within this frame of knowledge, it occurred to me that LGBTQ+ communities have reproduced the colonial legacy of sexual subjugation and repression by denying queer South Asians of access to reclaiming *our* queerness in diaspora. For this reason, I was deprived of my agency to construct—and be understood for—my culturally conducive identity as a queer South Asian womxn in LGBTQ+ spaces. This realization transformed my grief into rage.

Since the Western LGBTQ+ community promotes *living your truth*—a concept that was appropriated from Hinduism—I decided to move forward by doing exactly that. Thereafter, I would only live my truth.

Truth is: I am gay and I am South Asian and I refuse to be reduced to only one of these identities.

My blood boiled as I raised my psychological guard to protect my intersectional identity. I unabashedly and unapologetically asserted my integrated sexual, gender, and ethnic identities in LGBTQ+ spaces for purposes of challenging white queerness. I never missed an opportunity to ensure that queer South Asian voices were heard in white-normative LGBTQ+ spaces. I refused to accept a reality in which experiencing abysmal alienation, erasure, and pressure to shed one identity was common and normal for queer South Asian womxn. In spite of the safety risks associated with doing so, I was determined to combat the

collective invisibility of queer South Asian womxn—
unwilling to stop at anything.

The fact that both LGBTQ+ and post-colonial
South Asian cultures presently reject the other renders
my existence inherently political. It was impossible
for me to "turn off" my political consciousness. I
dedicated my life to collectively mobilizing queer South
Asian womxn in LGBTQ+ communities; albeit, to a
detriment. While rage-driven organizing allowed me to
push myself beyond human capacity, the intensity of
my rage clouded my foresight. Years passed before I
realized that my rage triggered me to raise my guard
so high that I was unable to experience contentment. I
was disappointed to realize that maintaining a constant
state of politically-charged rage towards the world
does not produce feelings of joy and self-love; rather,
it led to my severe burnout, which I furthered in the
name of passion.

The pain of being a queer South Asian womxn
reached its maximum when I lost functional ability as a
result of extreme burnout.

PART III: LOVE

Exile and burnout need healing. Passionate rage
as a coping mechanism only took me so far; there
was nothing to refuel me when I became depleted
of energy. Burning out barred me from enjoying all
the magical love around me. I failed to recognize that
it was possible for me to have a politicized identity
and depoliticized emotional connections. I hadn't yet
known that there was profound joy and healing to be

found in the moments of love and belongingness.

Queer South Asian Community Love

I have always been hyper-critical of queer spaces, as a result of feeling invisibilized therein. I refused to accept the possibility of experiencing joy therein. I overworked myself in pursuit of establishing community for queer South Asian diasporic womxn, in order to create joy for others; however, I deprived myself of such feeling by refusing to take breaks. In 2019, I was enlightened with a new perspective during the Pride March—one that would open a gateway to magical love and bliss.

Every June, I marched down the streets of Toronto in the annual Pride March wearing my shirt that reads "*Not All Lesbians Are White.*" This shirt allows me to challenge the hegemonic whiteness of queer spaces while feeling visible—if only for three hours each year—in a community that continually works to erase my existence as a queer South Asian. Scanning the crowds while marching forward, I recall seeing some faces light up as they pointed out my shirt to surrounding friends. A jolt of energy rushed through my body as we locked eyes. I ran over to these strangers, as if I were reuniting with lifelong friends after considerable time apart.

We simultaneously shouted, "another Desi?!" in excitement while embracing in what felt like one of the most liberating hugs of a lifetime. No introductions were needed; an instant connection was present within the few seconds of our interaction. After a lifetime of believing I was the only queer Brown person ever, it did not matter whether I was meeting the first or hundredth fellow queer Desi—it produced an identical feeling of intense and blissful happiness every time. I ran back to my spot in the Parade, radiating joyousness.

There is something immensely powerful about feeling seen as a queer South Asian. The irrepressible loneliness that consumed me for years finally escaped my soul. I felt valid. I cherish these magical encounters with unknown, yet familiar, queer South Asians, because these are the memories that allow me to begin healing the generational grief of queer erasure.

Queer South Asian Romantic Love

After a few negative dating experiences involving racist queer womxn, I raised my psychological guard up so high that I unintentionally conveyed an intimidating vibe, according to former romantic interests. The first time I let my guard down with a partner was amongst the most beautiful, transformative experiences I have lived.

I reminisce a warm summer night with my (then) partner, N.C.; we walked up and down the streets of Toronto's Gay Village with our fingers interlocked, sharing laughs and shy grins, before resting on a neighbourhood bench. She sat upright on the bench, glancing down at me often, as I laid my head on her lap with my body stretched out horizontally.

I quietly observed as she shared stories of her childhood and adolescent years as a queer Gujarati, laughing into a distance before warmly smiling down at my face, gently cuffing my right ear with her right hand.

Her eyes told me a familiar story of grief, anger, and pain, yet her tonal and body expressions conveyed otherwise.

I knew I was observing her unique and unspoken story of strength and resilience, which underpins the collective narrative of queer South Asian womxn. I couldn't help but smile as I felt the heaviness in my heart dissipate after nearly a lifetime of weighing me down. A feeling of bliss entered my heart and flowed through my veins, reaching every part of my body. A tear rolled down the side of my eye; this was a moment of pure joy, liberation, and self-acceptance. My heart enlarged with a pure and genuine feeling of love.

For once, it felt like I could just focus on being in love, without consciously and worryingly working to ensure my identity is understood before hesitantly moving forward. Perhaps it was the fact that N.C. and I shared the same Gujarati heritage that made it easier for me to love without my guard up; there was maximum vulnerability, comfort, and authenticity in our dyad. It was the kind of love that allowed me to recognize that I am worthy and deserving of love, as well as experience profound self-love and self-acceptance for all that I am. A wave of relief came over me as I realized, for the first time, that it is possible for me to romantically love someone without compromising any part of identity or anxiously anticipate violence[2] towards my identity

---

[2] Violence, in this context, refers to both deliberate and non-deliberate micro-aggressions and macro-aggressions.

as a queer South Asian womxn. My heart overwhelms with the exact feeling of joy that I experienced on the warm summer night, every time I reminisce.

This relationship was by no means perfect—there was certainly hurt in other parts of our time together. However, I pinpoint this moment as a marker of the best of what life could be. It was a moment when I could release myself of the chronic stress, grief, and rage of being a queer South Asian womxn, and feel the full depth of my emotions in all context. It was energizing and revitalizing, after years of being forced to shed either my queer or South Asian identity.

Finally, I had experienced what it is like to be loved and understood for all of my complex identities. Although my relationship with N.C. has ended, its magic will never fade. I hold these memories dear to my heart, because these are the feelings that facilitate my healing from my diasporic trauma of enforced assimilation to colonial notions of queerness.

PART IV: JOY

Being a queer South Asian womxn is an immensely heart-breaking experience; but in light of our stressful lives, there is joy to be found. For me, that joy is found in being a *Power Dyke*. I claim this title as a refusal to be disempowered by my oppressors, who have continuously tried to revoke my agency to define my sexuality because I am a Brown womxn.

While challenges remain in navigating my family front, the fact that my grief-turned-rage has furthered the collective visibility of queer South Asian womxn fuels my resilience. At the risk of my own safety, I actively construct spaces of belongingness for queer South Asian womxn in order to produce collective joy. It is the brief moments of authentic love and connection with fellow queer South Asians that continuously fill my heart with joy.

I finally achieved full self-acceptance when I reflected on my ability to experience authentic love with and within the queer South Asian community. Even when relationships are a cause of further struggle and pain, it is my ability to cherish these moments with the queer South Asian community that has kept me alive to this day. This joy is the reason I have held onto hope thus far.

I neatly folded each suicide note before placing them into a fresh manila folder labelled "PROJECT: INNER-PEACE." These notes, analyzed chronologically, told a story of growth and survivorship.

Rings and Other Shapes I've Known

Emily Win

When I was 12 years old, I convinced my parents to buy me a purity ring. It was 2007: *Tiger Beat* magazine, Disney Channel Original Movie CD-ROM soundtracks, jean skirts, and glitter lip gloss spilled out of my overstuffed closet drawers. In my eyes, the stars of preteen TV were infallible. Influential by design, their dramatic sitcoms, over-produced pop songs, and flashy inspirational heart-felt family value plot lines created narratives where a naïve 90's gal like me could feel intimately seen and understood.

During this pre-pubescent time one particular craze stuck to me most: wholesomeness, which was exuded most convincingly by the family-friendly Jonas Brothers. Claiming to never fall into the traps of the music industry, the boys made numerous public announcements regarding their personal decisions to stay chaste until marriage. My little tween heart beat out of my chest when I saw the boys defend their rings on the Teen Choice Awards broadcast.

My parents are technically Catholic, but they have never been self-proclaimed religious people. My siblings and I were baptized, confirmed, and indoctrinated into culturally Catholic activities and events, but political and personal issues alike were always taboo.

My mother gave me a piece of advice when I was too young to actually retain it: "Emily, when you start dating there are two subjects you should never talk about: religion and politics."

At the mere age of 10 I wondered about subtle peculiarities like why I was taught to look away from people holding "homeless please help" signs and knew it felt wrong to have "no opinion" during small talk with my friends' parents. These family-imposed restraints left me feeling ignorant and sad.

When I brought up the idea of getting a purity ring, I wasn't surprised when my parents responded with shrugged shoulders. A meek and gentle "Yeah sure, if that's what you think is best," was the most they could ever muster. They never had a sex talk with me, so all of my knowledge came from the Jonas Brothers fan page, occasional issues of *Seventeen*, and *The Care and Keeping of You*, published by the American Girl company. Despite my parents' indifference to the matter, I was gung-ho about using this flashy ring as leverage to fit in.

Unlike the Jonas Brothers' uniform, thick, inscripted chastity bands, mine was delicate; designed in faux silver embroidered with three hearts: one in the center for God and one on either side to represent the man and wife. Every morning I would brush my teeth, wash my face, and slide the silver-plated ring onto my ring finger with peppy devotion.

In my all-girls high school, I was the competitive athlete with unshaved body hair and a hidden yet raging anger against "the institution." Looking back this screams queer, but I somehow convinced my peers, friends, and even myself that I was pure as porcelain. To me, purity not only meant virginity, but a certain level of high academic and personal achievement-- an aesthetic that exuded the hopes of a heterosexual marriage and a white picket fence.

Within the privileged context of this private, Catholic institution, I yearned towards the world's greatest achievement a teenage girl at St. Ursula could aspire: The May Crowning Award. The young woman nominated, and democratically chosen as the girl to crown the Virgin Mary in May, was unequivocally accepted as a true servant of God, a real reflection of prudence, chastity, popularity and Christian love.

When I wasn't chosen, I spent many endless nights haunted by the rolodex of reasons why I was not enough. A friend who started a homeless outreach organization triumphed over me. As I watched her carry a white lacey veil down a makeshift aisle on our school volleyball court, I joined in the applause from other girls my age and school faculty who (rightfully) glorified her efforts. She placed the plastic crown atop a small ceramic head to the tune of "Hail Holy Queen" while I kept my rapidly pumping calf under control. Luckily my stimming was hardly noticeable, but my mind continued to endlessly pulse in waves of embarrassment and anger.

I was involved in every service activity, I helped with mass, and on occasion I even sang for the nuns across the street. Instead of having sex and going to parties, I studied hard, trained harder, and I attended every mission trip and retreat I could. On the outside I was excelling in all required areas. At our school, the essence of the "popular girl" held all of these aspects together. She could experiment, drink, and smoke, just as long as she could turn on the sophistication and class by 8 am Monday morning. The homecoming queen was always polished, well-spoken, generous, smart, diplomatic, and an expert at hiding a hangover. The key was in the façade.

During class I would twist the ring around and

play with the shiny band, hoping someone might catch me fiddling about and ask what it was: an evangelism tool I was all too familiar with. When the girls in my class showed no interest, I pivoted to see if the guys might be more impressed. I started reaching for the ketchup with my left hand while on dates, hoping the boy would ask a leading question. They never did, but I prided myself in keeping to a chaste lifestyle, knowing that everyone around me, including some divine figure up above, would award me for my efforts in Catholic socio-cultural conditioning.

Keeping the ring close meant holding tight to my perceived straightness. The ring was useful to ward off unwanted romantic and sexual advances from men. Even when the doctor insisted I get a cervical cancer vaccine, I refused retorting, "I absolutely will not be having sex until marriage."

The metal felt like a promise I could keep. I was safe, contained, nuclear. I could project the pinnacle idea of straightness while, in turn, gaining social clout: I could be "pure."

As birthdays passed my friends grew more comfortable experimenting with sex. None of the tales I overheard made the act of sex sound magical or like something that would make me stray from my purity promises. Some girls shrugged it off and played it cool, while others tried to keep it a secret, although the gossip always ran hot around school.

Everyone was doing it by senior year, but no one was talking to me about it as I had earned myself the title of the goodie-two-shoes. It was a reputation I was okay with. *At least I was following the rules.*

What I couldn't articulate at the time was that the thrill of my femme persona gave me the social power of my straight peers, while allowing me to secretly detest these hetero structures from a covert perspective. The ring gave me security in knowing I didn't have to face the "impure" thoughts I secretly questioned. It gave me the power to stay safely separate from my popular peers, while also protecting me from the parts of myself I wanted to ignore.

I enjoyed the social exhilaration of straightness and assumed the role of a public heterosexual. I invited boys to proms, I went on celibate dates, and I became obsessed with the idea of "FBO" (Facebook Official). Labels were my social pass into the world of religious belonging. The joy in pleasing my peers with straightened hair and pink manicured nails fulfilled me with the illusion of unconditional acceptance. More than anything, I wanted to fit in with girls who seem to have it all together: the skinny, white, girls with Christian bible studies and a ring before spring (a cultural phenomenon in the evangelical world where senior girls get proposed to by the Spring semester of their senior year).

I dated a few cisgender dude-bros. I reveled in the attention they gave me: a mixed-race "exotic" gal with the politics of a radical lesbian and the religious devotion of the Pope. None of them could really figure me out, and I think they liked the chase I gave them, playing the coy damsel when I made them wait for physical interaction.

In reality, this stemmed from a deep fear of kissing boys. When suitors showed interest, I would preface the date by warning them of my purity ring and "fear of kissing." One year, while working at a camp, I accepted the attention of a male counselor who had taken interest in me. This, I thought, was my chance to give heterosexuality a real go. Maybe I could force myself into straightness. Maybe this was the guy I had been looking for the whole time.

On one particular night with said suitor it became clear forced heterosexuality might not be possible for me: we sat on his bed when I could feel panic flooding my body and I blurted out "I want to become a nun!" He said it didn't bother him. He made some remark about wanting to kiss me. I looked down at my fidgeting hands and noticed the ring, hoping he would change his mind and we wouldn't have to kiss after all. Unsurprisingly, he didn't change his mind, and my body began to tense up as his tongue slowly moved into my mouth. My body was unyielding to his unwanted touch, and my fingers yearned for the magic of the purity ring to suddenly form a holy shield and repel him from my body. It felt like every inch of me yearned for release from this intimacy. And to my confusion, the ring hadn't worked, even on a mere kiss.

At the meek and budding age of 21 I signed up for an LGBTQ Literature class, just out of curiosity. A few of my college guy friends were gay males and I thought this would be good research, for their sake.

To my secret delight, the class was taught by a lesbian academic who wore clogs and asked prodding questions with a coy smirk. Halfway through the semester, she introduced the class to Alison Bechdel's *Fun Home*. I wasn't a huge fan of graphic novels, but

I enjoyed the literary genius of Bechdel's theoretical approach to heteronormativity. I had convinced myself that my fascination with queer theory was purely academic: the secrecy--the danger, the rebellion, the passion--the density and mystique of it all enticed my senses.

Reading *Fun Home* page by page, I felt a slow burn rising up from my gut. I loved looking at these graphics. The images and captions felt so familiar, so exciting, and so uncharted. One day we decided to read a large portion of the book in class. We reached the point in Bechdel's life where she started experimenting with her sexuality in college. The fire in my stomach began expanding as we flipped through scenes of Bechdel in striped turtlenecks, talking and flirting with various butch and femme characters. The heat within me blurred my vision--I hardly noticed anyone else in class, enraptured in the moment. As we approached the climax of the novel, Bechdel reads literature to her lover and my fingertips begin to tingle. Something about their naked bodies intertwined within queer theory felt peaceful. My body shook, and the pit in my stomach where a fire had earlier burned continued to haunt me the rest of the day.

A few weeks after my *Fun Home* encounter, I decided to enter a Catholic prayer night with the intention of sorting out my confusion. I had snuck into a conservative adoration night to spy on my right-wing peers and simultaneously get some alone time in a dark room filled with incense. I fell to my knees in front of the altar, shaking but determined, and asked God if I was queer.

. . .

Almost instantly, a gentle peace swept over me. As tears wet my cheeks, I began to laugh amidst the multitude of silent worshippers--almost as if I heard God say, "well, duh." I felt right, holy, and whole, maybe for the first time in my life. Coming out to myself at a religious service was going to be the only way I could see myself clearly. And, despite a collective hurt from the Church and years of confusion, I actually felt okay.

Even after coming out to myself and many of my peers, I knew the final step was looming. I needed to come out to my purity ring. It had been weighing heavy on my skin for far too long, begging me to let it breathe. Over the course of the 10 years it sat on my finger, the shiny silver complexion rubbing off, revealing its tarnished skeleton, reflecting the façade it had sustained in my life. I didn't want to let go of something so pure, fashioned, and established. Etched into the colloidal I felt the rules, the regulations, the romanticism of a wonder-bread packaged "God" wrapped around my veins every time I fingered the bumps and bends of a band not constructed to last.

A few years later, while living and serving in a Catholic intentional community, I decided to come out to a housemate of mine at the delicious but notoriously bigoted Chick-Fil-A. As the quiet hymns of evangelical praise played on the loudspeaker, she took a bite of her chicken sandwich and replied, "well, duh". She followed up with a sly, "me too."

We laughed, smiled, and joyfully yelled about little queer moments we both witnessed in one another throughout the course of living together. Both of us were raised in small-town Catholic Ohio, so we hungrily consumed every moment we could discussing our queer experiences: from small crushes we had, to our mutual appreciation for well-placed tattoos.

Finishing the last sips of our sweet lemonade, we decided we needed to mark our queer territory. We needed to do something to allow ourselves to be joyful, even happy about coming out of an oppressive Catholic lens and opening ourselves to a wider idea of sexuality, sex, and spirituality. Both of us had recently attended a Women's Retreat held by the local Christian parish, partly because we were curious and partly because we knew there would be free food. The retreat consisted of listening to a gaggle of millennials discuss their submissive roles to their men, informed by the Bible, and a brief overview of a book they gave us for free, titled "Don't Follow Your Heart," a nonfiction piece suggesting unchecked emotions were a path to the devil. We walked away from the afternoon with full stomachs but a newly found, furious passion to rid ourselves of this patriarchal nonsense.

Two nights before our volunteer program finished, we decided to hold a burn party for ourselves after the rest of our five housemates went to bed. By midnight we found ourselves sitting in our $5 Walmart kiddie pool in our bras and underwear talking about harmful theologies and envisioning new, inclusive, and even celebratory ways of perceiving the divine. To initiate our metanoia into this new philosophy, we gathered our evangelical "Don't Follow Your Heart" copies and burned them in our fire pit. As I ripped the pages out and tossed them in the blaze, I caught a flashy reflection from my ring finger. I paused, looked at my housemate, and took a deep breath.

I carefully gathered the last few ripped pages - about holy obedience - inserted them through the ring and fanned the edges out. The result looked like a napkin holder that encircles an elaborately folded white cloth napkin—the ones you see at wedding receptions. I took one last look at my ring and tossed it into the bonfire as my roommate yelled "Fuck the patriarchy. Fuck heteronormativity." I searched her eyes for affirmation. Standing in her sopping wet undergarments she congratulated me with a nod and a smile.

As we sat in our kiddie pool and continued our conversations about loves lost, we realized the fire hadn't burned all of the metal of the ring. Unwilling to let this deter me, I climbed out of the pool, found a hammer, and smashed it against our kitchen table. As much as I hoped this last-ditch effort destroyed the ring, the damage I inflicted only dented its malleable skeleton. In the spirit of peaceful negotiation, I decided to give it a final resting place in the hands of the St. Francis statue on our front porch.

It's been years since I last saw the ring. Sometimes I wonder if anyone picked it up, if an animal ate it, or if it's sitting among the flowers somewhere. I usually forget it existed.

Soon after, I evolved to a point where I yearned to question anything that tried to bind me. I wanted to trade my ring in for something less oppressive and more holistic, empowering, and joyful.

I now explore God in the ways my skin has grown dark over my ring-finger tan line. My sense of spirituality has less to do with that silver-plated circle and more to do with honoring the presence of life.

The empty space where my chastity was once guarded by the thin sliver of metal now welcomes a cool breeze or a lover's touch.

The empty space reminds me to celebrate the blank slate that is my queer body, owing gratitude to my own unique sacredness.

As I learn to accept my identity without that band of protection, I grow deeper in adoration of what my new spirituality could look like. A spirituality purged of objects and indulgences, of trinkets and societal trophies. A spirituality that is affirming, celebratory, sex-positive, and joyful.

I audibly thank God for rose gardens, chosen families, arts & crafts, the taste of a cool rosé in August, the freedom that comes with swimming naked in a lake, the feeling of orgasmic pleasure, the sensual way my skin interacts with other bodies.

Without the limitations and confinement of that poorly made band, my body can take on shapes it's never known.

The Ridiculous
Flamingo Dilemma

Aïda Yancy

I was not always the self-proclaimed Badass Black Queer Feminist Activist that I am today.

To be honest I worked very hard for years to be just the opposite.

I grew up as the only Black person and the only girl of my age in a tiny, tiny village, in a tiny, tiny country in Europe. Belgium, you might have heard of it? We have waffles, the original fries (don't call them French), and even chocolate thanks to the long and unspoken colonial history of that small spot on the map.

Growing up in that small town, my main goal in life was to make everyone forget I was different. My master plan required me to "fit in" by barricading myself in a locked closet.

FYI: it didn't work. I knew I was into girls. I had long known this truth and I was reminded of it regularly. But besides a dramatic and short-lived step out of the closet when I was seventeen, I did a pretty good job of pretending to be straight. I dated guy after guy to convince everyone, including myself, of my boring normalcy.

This strategy led me to meet the sweetest cis-white-straight-man with a non-overbearing masculinity complex I had ever met, marry him and have two children.

After my second child was born, I went back to college for my master's degree. The first year and a half mostly looked like a 9 to 5 student gig. I would get to campus around eight in the morning, drop off my then four-month-old at daycare, hop from the library, to my classes, to the daycare center to breastfeed my baby until it was time to go, pick her up, get home, pick up my son from school, cook dinner, feed my family of four, get the children to bed, crash in front of Netflix with my husband, go to bed, sleep, repeat. The constant activity of this routine left me constantly, slightly numb and with little time to worry about who I was and who I was meant to be.

I was studying History and at the end of my first year, was asked to choose an option. I would be lying if I said I had known what was waiting ahead; actually, at the moment, I nearly believed I had only chosen Gender Studies because the 18th century archives I was working on for my thesis mainly concerned women. Little did I know that it was the spark that led to the fire that made me reconsider my entire life.

My first assignment for Sociology of Gender was due before our very first class even started. I had to write an autobiography with this question as a theme: how did my gender influence my life? I took the assignment seriously and surprised myself by writing things I had never articulated before. Memories of traumatic events overcame me. I felt like I was going at my entire life with a fine-tooth comb and was picking up truckloads of gender and racially tinted events. By the time I was done writing, I couldn't ignore the discomfort I felt about my relationships with boys and then men. Of course, my "love life" was going to be questioned in such an assignment and what I found wasn't pretty. In the numerous dating experiences I had had in the course of my life before my husband, I couldn't find any that didn't feel wrong or abusive.

After handing in my essay, I thought about this and realized that I had never entered a single relationship with a man based on attraction, that they either started with a "friend becomes more" or a "I have something to prove myself" type of scenario and that in retrospect I had actually never asked myself the crucial question: "do I want to?"

I didn't realize that was something that mattered. It was what I was supposed to do, and what was expected of me. By digging, I realized I had received a "fast girl" reputation before I even had time to earn it.[3] I was a confused teenager at boarding school, feeling like a fox in a henhouse and ready to do anything to protect my cover. I had modeled my behavior after what people were projecting on me rather than what I was feeling and who I was.

I barely had time to digest this exercise that the semester started and my first class of Sociology of Inequalities put me on the stand. Literally. My professor helped us grasp the notion of privilege by making us line up on stage while he asked us some questions. We would step forward, step back or stay put depending on our answer. This Privilege Race is now very popular (and highly criticized) but at the time, it was a new experiment to me.

If you are a man, step forward.

If you are Muslim, take a step back.

If you are white, step forward.

---

[3] I was a Black girl in a white world after all, being oversexualized young is a story I have in common with many sisters. I just didn't know it at the time and had no one to open my eyes on the subject.

I saw everyone move back and (mostly) forth while I stayed put and even moved back. Soon I was far behind my fellow students with the only (white) hijab wearing Muslim girl of the class standing in front of me. My main privileges were to have a European passport (but so had everyone else on that stage) and to be married (take a step forward). That is when he said the one thing that really shook me:

If you are straight, step forward.

I lifted my right foot, ready to take the step but stopped mid-movement, leaving it awkwardly hovering in mid-air, swaying on my left leg, paralyzed.

Was I straight? I mean, I *was* in my third year of marriage and seventh year of relationship with a man, I *had* been very busy acting like the perfect wife and mother but...

Was I straight? To be fair, I had just written my gendered autobiography and things had emerged...

Was I straight?? Think quick, Aïda, you look like a ridiculous flamingo.

Was I straight??? I never called myself that, act quick, compromise!

I put my foot down next to the other and stayed where I was.

These two exercises turned out to be enlightening, emotional, and traumatic in many ways. They marked a spot that suddenly looked very much like the entrance of the legendary rabbit hole. I was suddenly face-to-face with all of the things I had tried quite successfully to keep out of my thoughts, truths that were hidden in an enormous dusty box in a secluded part of my mind. Keeping them out of sight was what granted me the security the hiding place that was my marriage provided. I was in the second half of my twenties and there were still so many parts of me that I was terrified to look at.

I started reading as much feminist theory as I could get my hands on, from Nicole-Claude Mathieu to Judith Butler as well as many authors on issues of Race and colonialism such as Edward Said or Gloria Wekker. Everything I was reading seemed to light a lightbulb in that dark and dusty part of my mind, making me reconsider the power dynamics in my household, in my family, and with my friends.

In every setting of my life, I was the only Black Woman surrounded by white, cis, straight people most of them being men.

In addition to the now constant state of challenge regarding my relationships, I also started struggling with self-perception. I realized how trapped I felt in the persona I had built, that respectable, perfectly conventional mother and wife persona.

I couldn't stand my clothes and my routine anymore. Everything felt asphyxiating, as if I were playing a part in someone else's fantasy life. I was in a permanent state of unrest, reconsidering my very position in this world in regard to my gender and my race. I was questioning my relationship with religion as a Muslim "by birth" who was forced to never show and practice early in life, and I was of course questioning my sexuality. I had opened the box and there was no closing it.

The first real sign of relief and revolution happened in the late spring of that year, in my bathroom, one morning. I was struggling through my new daily ordeal: getting dressed.

Either, I was too put together and wanted to tear my clothes off from the suffocation of it all, or I "looked weird" and couldn't make sense of what I was. Was I too modest, modest enough, strange, too Black, not Black enough, what was mine, what wasn't? My neurodivergent and slightly obsessive brain was torturing me, and I needed to justify what I had in front of me. *Who* was I? *What* was I? I knew I was sad, and angry, and confused, but what to do with all of that, where did I belong? And that's when the word popped in my mind: "QUEER".

Queer. I instantly calmed down; I said the word out loud repeatedly. *Queer.* Queer? Queer! Different inflexions, tones, speeds. Queer as an anti-category, queer as just me, queer as a place I can stretch and exist fully, queer as a promise that everything is possible, queer as a multitude, queer as liberation.

After I found that new way to express, describe, and comfort myself, I started giving myself permission. Explicit permission.

Permission to be myself always and foremost.

Permission to look, create, live outside the box.

Permission to explore.

Permission to hold some answers and seek others.

Permission to be radically honest with myself and the world.

Permission to look for and listen to my own desires.

Permission to mess up.

Permission to change, grow, evolve.

Permission to dream.

Permission to start again.

Permission to love.

I also found that giving yourself permission is one thing while managing to act on it is another entirely.

Allowing myself to explore and mess up, to escape the pressure of having to be the perfect conventional mother did help tremendously in how I was feeling about myself, but it obviously didn't stop all of the questioning going on. I was about to turn 27, and 27 was that age I had pictured as the time I would have figured *it* out, I *should* have figured it out.

Somehow, 27 sounded like adulthood to me and instead of enjoying what I had built I was questioning all of it, I didn't know what I wanted in life at the moment the fairy tales (and society) kept telling me I had achieved it all. I was married, a mom of two, and no one understood why I suddenly felt lost, wasn't this the *end* of the story? They got married, had many children and lived happily ever after. *The end.* And here I was, thinking of jumping ship.

To be honest, the dynamics at home were shifting and it wasn't only me. In the fall, the start of my second and last year of masters had coincided with my husband leaving academia, starting a new job, earning more money, and meeting new people. By the time spring arrived and my identity crisis started blooming with the local flowers, my sweet husband started acting strange. He would have more and more engagements in the evenings, offer to take the kids to the park or the museum on his own, spend hours on end on his phone including during meals and family events. It didn't take me long to realise that he had fallen in love with someone else.

When I confronted him, he quickly confessed, and promised me no one had acted on it. But as time passed it became apparent that he kept seeing her, often prioritizing his "friendship" with her, and the friends they had in common, over time with me. But as I was feeling more and more unwanted, I also found more space to wonder and explore what I wanted. I started having a social life again, living my life without him. We had met during our Bachelor's program in University and we shared all of our friends. Most of our social gathering involved the same two other couples and I hadn't ventured out of that circle for years. I started going out more, to academic events, conferences, for a drink with fellow students. Soon we started communicating via calendar:

"I'm not home Thursday evening, are you?"

"If you aren't home tonight, I asked my sister and she's very excited to take the kids."

We were seeing less and less of each other even though we were still sharing a home and a bed, post-it notes and kind words, *Game of Thrones* evenings with friends, and family gathering.

We were just very respectfully drifting apart.

After close to a year of self-exploration leading me to territories farther and farther from my husband, I had nearly gone through my entire list of identity crisis topics:

Race: check!
Class: check!
Gender: check!
Religion: check!

The next one on my list was the one I was the least comfortable approaching because it was the one that would have the most consequences. But I couldn't ignore it for much longer, not when it was nudging at me increasingly often. I had been attending queer events and making friends that made me feel safer than I had ever felt. So, I started seriously thinking about my sexuality. I had accepted I was into women and non-binary people; I was purposefully ignoring the bit of myself asking if I was into men at all. I ended up proposing an open marriage to my husband and see where it would lead us. I remember that conversation to have been very honest and matter of fact:

Me: Hmmm, you know how, when we fight, I keep saying that next time, I'll certainly not choose a cis-white-straight-man as a partner?

Him: Yeah…

Me: And how clearly, the person you keep texting day in, day out is getting more and more important to you?

Him: yeah *looks puzzled and wonders where I'm getting at*

Me: I wondered if it would make sense, and even be healthy for us, to give each other some space to explore on our own…

Him: Ok

Me: I mean… maybe we could have an open marriage for a while, make sure we use protection if it comes to that

Him: Ok…

Me: As long as we are honest with each other

about our feelings and make a point not to share
any detail (that would be uselessly painful)
Him: Ok.

I had developed a crush on a girl that was
frequenting the same spaces I was, and that crush was
growing. When my husband and I agreed to open our
marriage, this forbidden crush became more then shy
flirtation. I felt so alive! I had no memories of such
butterflies. And a couple of weeks later, a weekend of
activism gave us the perfect opportunity to spend the
weekend together, nights included.

I remember that weekend as it had all happened
yesterday. That first night, the intimacy of sharing the
twin bed of her student room, the whispered words
in the dark, the joy and pleasure of not being able to
keep our hands off each other. The second night, in
a bigger bed, in a bigger room lent to us by a friend.
There was a postcard on the door of that bedroom
with two otters holding hands on it. It read *Will you be
my significant otter?* In that soft white bed, I finally said
the words I had never dared to. That night feels like a
river in my memory, the flow of words unstoppable
through the night. As if a huge ball of yarn had been
forgotten behind boxes on the highest shelf and that
reaching for something else, we had unsettled it and it
had fallen, unravelling through the room. I will forever
be grateful to her for having been there to catch me
and my words at that moment, to receive all these
things that had been hidden, ignored, inside of me. In
my memories, I gave her my entire life story, curled up
against her, my head in the fold of her shoulder, my

face close to her breast, starting from the beginning. All the little steps that had led to that very moment, all the heartache, the violence, the abandonments and then the joys. I don't think I had ever had anyone welcoming me and listening to me with that purity and acceptance before. I don't think I've spoken like this since. That weekend unlocked something enormous in me. It broke down all of the last barriers inside of me, and once that was done, there was no going back. Lying to myself was not an option anymore, and neither was continuing my life as I had led it.

I arrived home that March Sunday evening to my husband washing the dishes. When I offered to help, he knew something was up (I *DON'T* do dishes if I can avoid it). Standing in the kitchen, I explained to him that I had had a very eye-opening realization, and crying and apologizing, I told him: "I am a lesbian."

An hour or so later, we were sitting close together on the couch, my head on his shoulder, quietly and tenderly dividing our possessions, a glass in hand. His reaction when I told him was to hug me. We hugged for a while, half crying, half laughing. He then fixed us two loaded Gin and Tonics and said: "You take the *Harry Potters*, I'll take the *Game of Thrones.*"

Everything went very fast from there. My very spontaneous coming out, was followed by what felt like an endless suite of announcements to our friends, close colleagues and family. We were having a divorce, no it wasn't anyone's fault, yes you could stay friends with him, I am a lesbian, the kids are fine.

For some reason, that is the one question EVERYONE asked. How are the kids???? As if they would be traumatized that their own mother might be a lesbian. I jokingly explained to everyone that the children were still too young to know that divorce was very officially one of the first signs of the apocalypse and that they had not yet completely integrated norms about heterosexuality. This, of course, was true. They had taken the news with the matter-of-fact way only toddlers and 5-year olds are capable of.

Imagine: it's early spring, the weather is beautiful, the four of us are in the living room, and we, the adults, are trying to have the kids sit quietly on the couch. Of course, Miss Toddler is fidgeting and it takes a while to get her to sit. 5 year old is sitting upright in the most unchildlike, serious clerk-like posture.

Mom, bracing herself: *Breathes deeply*, Kids, we need to tell you something...
5 year old, still in his clerk upright position: Yes? What?
Mom: Daddy is going to move out.
5 year old: Really... Why?
Mom: Because mom and dad are separating *suspenseful silence, Mom and dad exchange a look*
5 year old: Ok... Why?
Mom: Because mom and dad are not in love anymore
5 year old: But... Why?
Mom: Because mom likes girls
5 year old: Ah, ok.

To his little mind this was settled. Mom was a girl, Dad was a boy. Mom liked girls, Dad was still a boy. CQFD.

At least the children were doing well. On my side, even if I was actually ecstatic to get to live a life I only had secretly fantasized about and thought impossible, the entire separation process was extremely emotional. There were thousands of pragmatic arrangements to be made (who is going to live where, with what, when, …), I was swamped at work and it didn't help that I had uncovered the truth hours before sharing and thus had had 0 time to process what had and what was happening. On the bright side I had suddenly received a freedom I had never had before, and I had never thought possible again, or at least not before my children's majority.

I rearranged my entire apartment in a way that gave me the impression of having a new place. I had gained custody of the cat and the kids were now staying with me a week out of two. This exhilaratingly meant that I was now childless, single and living alone half of the time (talk about a rewind button!) while being really able to focus on them the other. I had the best of both worlds, and the kiddos seemed so much happier now that there were no micro-tensions at home between their parents.

Accepting my queerness was the key to my freedom, although, at the time, I had no idea of how much it would shape my future. Living outside of that box, in my full very personal type of flamboyance, offers me joy in the most authentic ways. That year had its lot of challenges and hardships, I notably ended up violently burning out and leaving my exploitative job by September. But even through all of the pain and exhaustion, I have no regrets. This was years ago now, and I have never felt this happy. I am now a nearly fulltime activist, I work for an LGBTQI+ NGO where I get to focus on what really matters to me such as issues of race, gender, sexualities and social inequities. I have moved, adopted a second cat and I may even be living my best love story ever.

Hot Sand, Beach Plums, and Elvira

James Finn

I never told Lenny, but a cute boy sent me flying through the air, sliding and scraping across hot asphalt.

Oh, he knew about the hot asphalt part. How not? My back and left thigh erupted in road rash, a phrase I didn't even know back then in my callow youth. How I avoided cracking my skull, I'll never know. I bounced it good a couple times.

I'd blame it all on Cassandra Peterson, better known as Elvira, Mistress of the Dark, but that wouldn't be fair. I swear she didn't push me.

Maybe I should start over, because this is a love story, reader, and it certainly isn't sounding like one.

Have you been to Provincetown? It's a lovely little village at the very tip of the Curly-Q tail of Cape Cod.

Think white sand, slippery dunes, fierce wind, beach plums, and icy Atlantic currents.

Think Portuguese bakeries, rusty fishing fleets, lobsters, and clam bakes. Think hot boys and afternoon tea dances at the Boat Slip!

Oh, yes, P-Town bustles with cute boys in speedos. In season, it's "gay as," and it has been for decades.

Lenny was my big lug of an Alphabet City Lothario

My husband in all but legal reality, he was a generation older than me, twice as large, and three times as gruff. If not for that smile that lit him up like a bonfire, he might have made you nervous. His Lower East Side accent grumbled straight out of a *Godfather* movie.

But when he laughed! His sparkling eyes told the rest of the story. Lenny was "out and proud" before Stonewall. He just couldn't help it. His voice never lost its masculine edge, but it dripped with the promise of

135

so much more. He reveled in camp femininity.

Is that how Leonard Bernstein recognized him one night? Slowed the car on a dark side street near Lincoln Center and beckoned Lenny to get in? "Only if you want to, handsome." Maybe. That's how Lenny tells it.

I like to think it's true

I like to think I've made love with a man who made love with one of the world's phenomenal composers and conductors. New York is magical like that, when you're young. Six degrees of separation melt into one, and probability precipitates like rain falling out of a clear sky.

I know it's true that Lenny met Cassandra Peterson at a gay bar in the West Village years before I came along. I've seen the pictures! Before she made the Elvira character famous, they hung out on Fire Island and mixed clam juice cocktails with cranberry and too much vodka.

They took to renting a convertible and tooling away to P-Town at the end of August, every summer. Little did I know, lounging around with my college buddies, laughing at her movie commentary, that she and my future husband were already fast friends.

Little did I know she'd send me flying over the handlebars of a mountain bike!

But I'm not writing about Elvira, Mistress of the Dark. I'm writing about my love affair with Lenny. He startled me out of sadness one afternoon as I sat reading the New York Times at the LGBT Center in Greenwich Village. I call him "the biggest plot twist of my life."

I was alone in the City, just finished with a stint in

the military, quickly burning through what I had left of a healthy savings and scared to death I'd have to drag my sorry ass back to the heartland, tail between my legs.

When he tapped my newspaper and grinned at me on a dare, my universe shifted dimensions. "That's it!" he growled like a Bowery Boy. "I knew you'd be much cuter if you didn't look so sad."

Our affair burned hot and passionate for weeks

Plays off off Broadway. Musicals. Performance Art. The Real New York. Lenny's Real New York, which quickly became mine. Opera in the park with kosher deli and cheap Italian wine in paper bags. Salty pickles and cheesecake for dessert.

I'd lay my head on his chest and he'd run his fingers through my wispy blond hair as we thrilled to Puccini and Verdi. Sometimes the metallic drum clicking up into my ear kept time to the music, often it didn't.

"What's that?" I asked him the first time I heard it. "Your chest clicks."

He shook his head slowly from side to side. "Nuthin'. Mitral valve. Artificial. Not important." For the first time since we met, I could hear the lie in his voice, but I didn't push him.

Joint bank accounts, joined hearts, and a cat

Came the day we adopted a little cat. I'd already moved in; it just made sense. I had a job he helped me find, so why waste my pay on rent when we spent every minute together?

Our little grey tiger sealed the deal in our hearts. We became family. "I love you" felt normal and natural, almost as natural as that clicking I'd still hear every night as we lay naked, limbs intertwined, my head nested in his hairy chest, sleep lulling us both.

We walked to the bank together one bright day, ready to join our finances. Take out a joint savings account and add my name to his checking. "Stop here," Lenny ordered, pulling out a white wicker chair at the sidewalk cafe across from our marble-pillared destination.

"Huh? We just had coffee." I sat and thumbed the menu, put off by the sober tone in his voice.

He waved the waiter off and looked me in the eye. "Look... before we do this? I haven't been honest with you. Not in any way to hurt you, but ... if we're gonna take this step, you gotta know somethin'."

That's when he explained the clicks

"I don't know exactly how long," he sighed. "But I'm not ... That artificial mitral valve? It's really important. And so is my pacemaker. My heart ain't right, hasn't been since I was born. You gotta know what you're gettin' into wit me, kid."

So, he told me the whole story. And I listened, and I KNEW. I tell myself I didn't, but he explained every last detail years before he died exactly the way he told me he would die. With the optimism of youth, I denied it all, shut it all up in a little box inside my chest and threw the key away.

Because love wins. All the stories say so.

That last time we rented a little red convertible and tooled to P-Town together, everything was already changing anyway. Tilly, the vivacious Portuguese grandmother Lenny had been renting the cottage from for 20 years, had shrunk and faded.

What was it? Our sixth summer there? Seventh? Enough I felt at home. Last week of August, first week of September every year. Beach plum jelly on Portuguese rolls with fresh brewed coffee as the sun rises. That's P-Town for me.

Did you know you can watch the sun rise and set from the same beach, way out on the tip of the cape? Try it sometime with somebody you love. Remember that jam. Sunrise tastes so much better with it.

"I won't be renting next summer," Tilly growled as we unpacked at the little red-tiled cottage. "Too much work. Too tired. I'm sorry, Lenny."

He looked as exhausted as she did, pale and slow. I grabbed the suitcase from him and made him sit on the rocker out in the breeze while I folded his shirts into tight wooden drawers.

He'd become an old man just as fast as he told me he would. Those clicks hadn't been lying. But, oh the fun we had! I rented a mountain bike like I always did. Spent the mornings biking the dunes and swimming in icy surf. Packed lunches and sipped sparkling water while he strolled downtown, shopped, gossiped, and searched out dinner spots.

Afternoons meant naps, books, lovemaking, and quiet talk. Evenings unrolled like formal dates. A different fabulous restaurant with artsy food and overpriced wine. Cute waiters and gay culture. "Oh, sweetie!" Lenny might gush to the busboy. "Don't you live in the west 20s? Didn't we see you at that opening at the Joyce last spring?"

Strolling back to Tilly's cottage might involve a cranberry cocktail or possibly an ice cream. But strolling back that summer, those last two weeks we ever spent in P-Town, was hard. Lenny was exhausted most every day and fighting to breathe. By sundown, he was just done.

We cut our evenings short, and he had to lean on me on the way back.

One night, Tilly was rocking on the porch as we turned the corner. "Lenny!" she called. "Lenny! Guess who wants you on the phone!"

Elvira was on her way. Mistress of the Dark.

She was flying into Boston and wanted to know if Lenny had the usual cottage at the usual time. Could she run up the Cape and say hi for old time's sake? She'd get a room if she could find one, but she might have to crash with us.

Lovemaking in the afternoon. Did I really write that?

Lenny and I had a lot of sex. Until we didn't anymore. When he started to smell like hospitals and medicine, I got scared. His physical state messed with the denial I needed to stay optimistic.

We'd go weeks without sex, and I felt guilty, because I knew it was my fault. I'd ignore subtle hints on his part, and once we did get going and he had trouble responding, I'd stop pretty damn quick. I loved him, but his sickness made me shrink and shrivel. I didn't want it to, but it did.

We'd always made love in the afternoons in P-Town, but not that last summer.

Waiting for Elvira

I took the bike out the next morning and pumped up and down dunes, reveling in my health, my strength, the power in my limbs and abs. I was young, fit, bronzed, and ... horny.

I hadn't had sex with Lenny since we arrived, but the hot sun and all the hot boys had me in a state. I was agitated, and I was feeling guilty about it. I knew which dunes out at Herring Cove were the right dunes for a quick blow job. I pedaled past them twice. Three times. Maybe four.

But I'd pushed Lenny away the afternoon before, and I couldn't bring myself to stop the bike and cruise. It felt wrong, selfish, even though I knew Lenny wouldn't mind as long as I told him about it. That was our rule.

Cassandra was on the way, probably driving up the Cape already, so I headed back.

I saw him on the trail ahead of me, gorgeous. Sun glinting all glossy blue off raven-black hair. He was shirtless, sweating, and too beautiful to be true. I raced ahead and rode beside him. "Hi, come here often?"

We started to race, and when we reached the parking lot, it was on. All that smooth asphalt after sandy trails? We jetted ahead, glorying in athletic speed, laughing. I knew I had to get to know him. It couldn't end here.

All I could think of was Elvira

"She's coming here!" I shouted as I looked back at him over my shoulder. "The Mistress of the Dark! You have to stop by the cottage and ..."

I never saw the speed bump. I never felt the collision. One moment I was planted in my seat, the next flying through the air, describing a perfect parabola that seemed to arch on forever. I remember thinking how hard the ground looked, right before I hit, skidded, and thumped my skull.

I was too dizzy and sick to bike home. Somebody put me in a jeep and drove me. I never saw raven-hair boy again. The jeep wasn't his.

Lenny gasped to see me covered in blood, but I assured him it was all superficial. I lay on our bed, fought not to vomit, and urged him to go into town and find Elvira.

"Oh, Cassandra? Her flight got delayed and she decided she didn't have time for P-Town after all. She might make it out to the Hamptons for Thanksgiving. We'll see."

He went over to Tilly's for dinner and brought me some back. Something with clams and pasta that I was too sick to eat.

Two afternoons later, Lenny handling me gingerly because of all the damage, we finally did make love. The last time we ever did in Provincetown, and close to the last time ever.

Why then? Maybe my injuries put me on par with him somehow. Maybe feeling sick and weak changed my mindset. Or maybe I'm blaming myself too much, and we were just lucky that afternoon that everything came together.

I buried myself in his hairy chest after, holding him tight, listening to that click echo endings into my ear. "I love you," I whispered. "Forever."

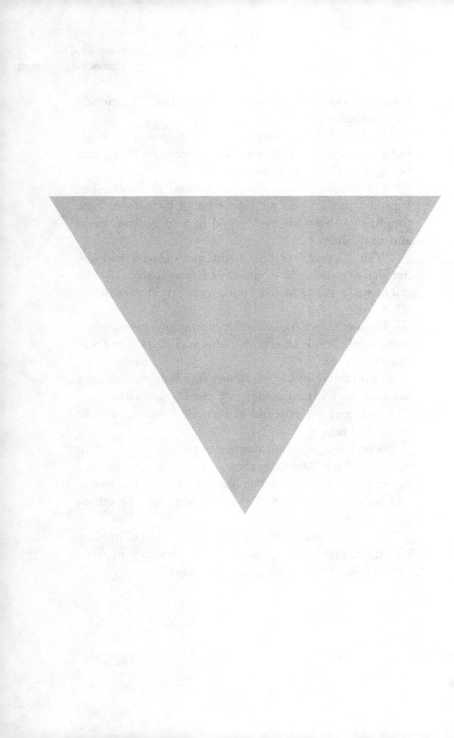

Handsome
and
Belly Kisses

Rachel Wiley

Handsome

At the store where we have stopped
to buy the candy we will sneak
into the movies on date night, the cashier greets us with a smile,
compliments my dress, says I look so pretty tonight
before wondering out loud why my date isn't also dressed up,
as though she isn't standing right next to me,
paying for the candy,
doesn't she want to be pretty too?
I cannot stop the giggle that erupts from my startled throat
at witnessing what could only be this grown woman's first ever
sighting of a real live butch
in the wild.

My date doesn't want to be pretty,
she doesn't need to want to be pretty
to be a woman. She is a woman because she tells me so.
She is a woman because there is no wrong way to woman.
She is a woman on her terms; a woman with the lump of a soft
leather billfold in her back pocket, who holds my doors and doesn't
mind that my grandma calls her a little gentleman, wears a pair of
boxer briefs better than most men and is the only person I've ever
called daddy.
A woman, who is often tipped less than the flirty femmes on
the wait staff she manages, because her not pretty makes people
uncomfortable.
My date was dressed up for date night; wearing a dress shirt/a
slightly loose necktie/pants that I'm almost certain she ironed.
When she picked me up from my house, I swooned at the cuffs of
her shirt rolled to her elbows/her tattoos peeking out/ a hint of

things under the dress shirt I would trace my fingers along later.

In a similar such-moment of fingers sliding along skin I called her beautiful.

She buried her face into my neck and politely refused it, said it wasn't her word

and still she remains a woman,

a woman who grins and blushes an entire sunset when I shyly tell her she is handsome-

the most handsome sunset I've ever seen.

Belly Kisses

There is a beautiful woman in my bed.
After a lot of awkward flirting
we started kissing on my couch
then made our way up to my bedroom
auxiliary articles of clothing
(cardigans, leggings, socks) peeling away
until all that remains between our skins are our simple dresses.
My first instinct any time my dress is pulled over my head
is to wrap my arms across my belly
less in shame
and more a shield from the disgust the world
constantly promises for it.
I love my body more days than I don't and that is a long
won battle,
but asking anyone else to love my body still sometimes
feels like asking too much.
Every time I've let someone fuck me with my dress still on
I laid in bed afterwards
and vowed that I would not let another person inside me
that hasn't seen me fully - not just seen but marveled at
and pressed their lips to the parts deemed unworthy
a promise I break every time the need to be touched
outweighs the need for dignity
I am still learning how to ask for what I deserve without it
also sounding like an apology
When at last I hold my breath and plunge from my
dress into open air
There is a beautiful woman waiting on the other side,
And unasked she presses her lips to my belly

before I can reach to cover it.
And She marvels,
And She runs her hands over all of me like her palms
might just sluff the world's cruelty from my skin
There is this beautiful woman in my bed
and she holds beauty the same way I hold beauty
hard won with both hands, overflowing
When she emerges from the poly/cotton undertow
of her own dress
How can I help but love her body the same way
I have fought every day to love my own?
And now I kiss, I marvel, I reach
& her body answers my wanting hands
She is endless
We are both so endless and unshielded
and weightless here
in my bed
Weightless
But not the least bit smaller
thank God not the least bit smaller

Afterword

Samantha Mann

In 2019 I had the opportunity to read a portion of my essay collection, *Putting Out: Essays on Otherness*, at George Mason University's annual Fall for the Book festival. I was sponsored by the gender studies program and despite it being a room full of my kinds of folx, feminists, queers, truth seekers, and literary nerds, I was apprehensive. It was my first time reading my work out loud and I was nervous to fill 60 minutes talking about myself. The whole thing felt a little self-indulgent and embarrassing, so I created activities for the students to do that correlated with my reading's selections and then at the end I forced them to share various experiences out loud. I would not be presenting alone!

As I listened to the students talk about their own experiences of otherness, I was stunned at their vulnerability and individual use of language. On the spot these students were creating prose and building connections through their varied but shared experiences. I wished I had recorded them. It was obvious, even if I wanted to, I would never be able to write their stories; they weren't mine. Even at my best, I would only ever be imitating them or at worst perverting their one-of-a-kindness. Right away I wanted to scoop them up and place them in a writing workshop. As I rode the train back to Brooklyn that night it was clear; I needed to put together an anthology.

I wanted to create a space for story-tellers and professional writers alike. Too often there is a differentiation in who gets to tell stories and what kinds of stories should be grouped together, poetry collections versus essay collections versus narrative fiction. I wanted all of the people and all of their modes in one location.

When I began reaching out to various artists and story-tellers I either knew personally or those who caught my attention online another thing was clear; I was craving community. Unfortunately, my life had not turned out to be like *The L Word*. While I had queer friends, I still longed to feel closer to more queer people.

As I began to edit stories and learn about the creators, I found I was understanding more about my own experiences and seeing how even though many of us had disparate upbringings many truths were illuminated. Growing up a queer child can feel especially isolating, especially when you don't know why. "It is so nice to connect to other queer adults, who were once kids and realize that I was never really alone" writer Danny G. Roy wrote to me one night. We always had each other even though we didn't know. It seemed like we were all looking for deeper connections. After a year of prodding and wrangling this group I sat with the full collection and it felt like we had created a home. The writers don't know each other and haven't seen one another's stories and yet the pieces felt familial.

Editing this collection combined with getting to know this group of queer people have tampered some of my survivor's guilt that lingered at the start of this project. In February 2021 I had the immense pleasure and honor to interview J.E.B. (Joan E. Biren) about the rerelease of her photography anthology *Eye to Eye: Portraits of Lesbians*. During our conversation

I described this guilt using the term "privileges" to describe my life (being legally married, embraced by family, having my name on my son's birth certificate).

J.E.B. listened and responded, "Feling guilty isn't stupid, but it is a total waste of time and energy. And the reason is, because the things you're talking about are not privileges. They're rights. And everybody should have those rights. And if nothing had changed from my time to yours, then everything we were working toward would have been in vain, and that would have been horrible. And the fact that you can do all that actually makes me joyful. And you know, it's not that I don't understand survivor's guilt. I'm 76 years old, a lot of my friends have died. A lot of my friends who are younger than me have died. So, I get it. I'll tell you how I deal with it. Every day, when I wake up, I say to myself, okay, today, let's try to bring some goodness in the world, no matter how small and contribute something useful."[1]

I hope this anthology can be something of use to us all.

---

[1] Mann, Samantha. "Looking at the Groundbreaking 'Eye to Eye: Portraits of Lesbians," March 12, 2021, BUST, https://bust.com/books/198021-jeb-joan-e-biren-eye-to-eye-portraits-of-lesbians-interview.html.

@TheBrooKlynBruja
TheBrooKlynBruja@gmail.com

I Feel Love Contributors

Sdmann0502@gmail.com
Samantha Mann

Río Alvia
Río is a mental health advocate using poetry and collaged surrealism art to challenge the binary, destigmatize Borderline personality disorder and to advocate for human and non-human rights.

John DeLamar
John DeLamar grew up in small town Georgia, and followed the bright lights of Broadway to New York City. He can be found directing plays and musicals or teaching English at the Brooklyn School for Music of Theatre when not locked away writing.

James Finn
James Finn is a former Air Force intelligence analyst, long-time LGBTQ activist, an alumnus of Queer Nation and Act Up NY, an essayist occasionally published in queer news outlets, and an "agented" novelist.

María García
María Fernanda García Lozano is a multipotentialite who never sits still. She lives in NYC because it allows her to be anything and everything; from a UX Researcher, to a Flamenco dancer, to a writer, to a blockchain enthusiast. When she is not working, she plays house with her partner in their cute little

apartment in Jackson Heights.

Greg Mania

Greg Mania is the author of the memoir *Born to Be Public*. His words have been published in *The New Yorker, Vanity Fair, O, The Oprah Magazine, PAPER,* among other international online and print platforms. He lives in Brooklyn.

Esther Mollica

Esther Mollica has written for *Wired, GO Magazine* and *Autostraddle*. Her short romantic comedy, *Never the Bride*, was featured as one of four films by up-and-coming women of color in San Francisco's Frameline Film Festival, 2010.

Sonali Patel

Sonali (Alyy) Patel is a trailblazing LGBTQ+ researcher, community organizer, influencer, writer, and activist, who has made monumental strides for Queer South Asian Women. Patel pioneered research on Queer South Asian Women's issues in Canada, founded the Queer South Asian Womxn's Network—a thriving national organization—and recently, made LGBTQ+ history as the first South Asian speaker of Pride Toronto's Dyke March.

Danny Roy

Danny Roy is a mental health care worker living for some time in the Pacific Northwest—though recent long jaunts to the California desert have begun to conjure fantastical new possibilities. The plumpest, most yellow Marigold will always be his favorite flower in the patch.

Sara Sugar-Anyanwu
Sara Sugar-Anyanwu is a former journalist turned SEO expert and start-up junkie. She lives with her wife and rescue doodle in Ditmas Park, Brooklyn. When she's not cooking or hanging with her wife and pup, she's working on her first novel — a queer post pandemic thriller.

Rachel Wiley
Rachel Wiley is a queer, biracial poet and performer from Columbus, Ohio. She is a fellow and faculty member of the Pink Door Writing Retreat held annually for women and nonbinary writers of color in upstate New York. She has performed at slam venues, colleges, and festivals nationwide.

Her first poetry collection, *Fat Girl Finishing School*, was first published in 2014 by Timber Mouse Publishing and rereleased by Button Poetry in June 2020. Her second collection, *Nothing is Okay*, was published in March 2018 by Button Poetry and received the 2019 Ohioana People's Choice Award. Her forthcoming collection, *Revenge Body*, is set to release in January of 2022.

Emily Win
Emily (she/hers) is a Midwesterner by nature, but now enjoys writing and podcasting about queerness and spirituality from her Los Angeles apartment. She

currently works in education management and does freelance writing, editing, teaching, and podcasting on the side. In her "free time" she's DIY crafting, forming QPOC community, or collaging. Follow her on all socials @_erosececilia

Aïda Yancy

Aïda Yancy is an Antiracist, LGBTQI+ Feminist activist based in Brussels, Belgium. Her work and research bring her to focus on issues of intersectionality and safe(r) spaces for multi-marginalized people. In her free time, she reads, knits, and sews.

A Note to our Furious Readers

From all of us at Read Furiously, we hope you enjoyed our latest anthology collection, *I Feel Love: Notes On Queer Joy.*

There are countless narratives in this world and we would like to share as many of them as possible with our Furious Readers.

It is with this in mind that we pledge to donate a portion of these book sales to causes that are special to Read Furiously. These causes are chosen with the intent to better the lives of others who are struggling to tell their own stories.

Reading is more than a passive activity – it is the opportunity to play an active role within our world. At Read Furiously, we wish to add an active voice to the world because we believe any growth within the company is aimless if we can't also nurture positive change in our local, national, and global communities. The causes we support are designed to encourage a sense of civic responsibility associated with the act of reading. Each cause has been researched thoroughly, discussed openly, and voted upon carefully by our team of Read Furiously editors.

To find out more about who, what, why, and where Read Furiously lends its support, please visit our website at readfuriously.com/charity

Happy reading and giving, Furious Readers!

Read Often, Read Well, Read Furiously!

To read more of Samantha
Mann's work, please check out:

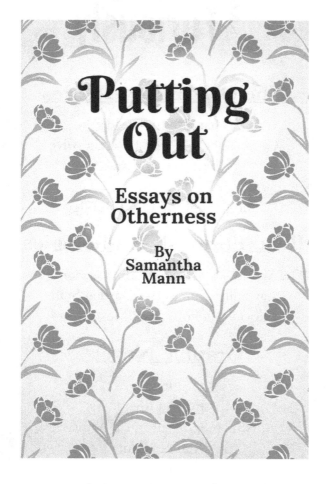

Putting
Out

Essays on
Otherness

By
Samantha
Mann

Look for these other great titles from

The One 'n Done Series

What About Tuesday
Girls, They'll Never Take Us Alive
Brethren Hollow
Helium
The Legend of Dave Bradley

Read Furiously Anthologies

The World Takes: Life in the Garden State
Stay Salty: Life in the Garden State
Furious Lit vol 1: Tell Me A Story

Graphic Novels

Firsts
Northwood Meadows
Pursuit: A Collection of Artwork
In the Fallout
Brian & Bobbi
The MOTHER Principle

Fiction

A Parade of Streetlights
Chasing Harmony
Working Through This

Non-Fiction

Cars, Castles, Cows and Chaos
I Feel Love: Notes on Queer Joy
Nerd Traveler
We don't do "just okay" anymore
Putting Out: Essays on Otherness

Kid's Titles

The Little Gray Witch
The Boy Who Wasn't A Witch

Poetry

All These Little Stars
Silk City Sparrow
Dear Terror
Whatever you Thought, Think Again
Until the Roof Lifted Off